Life Balance

Love Your Life by Finding Mental, Physical, Emotional and Spiritual Abundance.

Rodolfo Menjivar

DEDICATION

This book is dedicated to you. To the one reading this. I wrote this for you in hopes that you are able to find something within these pages that will help you move forward in life. Hopefully it will also open you up to a new perspective on what it means to be healthy. Thank you for saying yes to moving forward in your journey to a healthy lifestyle.

CONTENTS

Acknowledgments   I

Introduction   Pg #3

1 Mindset   Pg #7

2 Meditation and Yoga   Pg #18

3 Food and Water   Pg #27

4 Exercise   Pg #42

5 Emotional I.Q.   Pg #53

6 Trust   Pg #67

7 Spirituality   Pg #81

8 The Signs   Pg #95

9 God   Pg #108

10 Balance   Pg #119

Conclusion   Pg #131

ACKNOWLEDGMENTS

There are so many people I would like to thank that I could write a book just based on that. I would like to thank everyone that has cheered me on through this process. You all gave me the energy and motivation to keep pushing on the days that I wanted to quit. I would like to thank Annie, my editor, without whom this book would not have been finished. Most importantly, I would like to thank my mom! Without her I would have never made it this far in life and I don't even want to think of where I would have ended up.

Introduction

The Life Balance book is designed to be an introduction on how to start leading a healthy lifestyle. It will help people get one foot in the door of living a healthy life.

It will help you begin to understand what being healthy really means and what it takes to get there. It will give you the necessary information and tools to get you started and to keep you moving forward.

The book will take you through what I feel are the four major areas of life. The mental, physical, emotional and spiritual. I feel that each of these areas play a big role in our overall health. Health has to do with a lot more than just the physical aspects of exercise and what we eat.

I will start by discussing our mental health as I feel that without a healthy mind and mindset we will not get very far in our journey towards health. We must be able to filter out the negative influences in our mind and fill it with positivity and reaffirming words. Our minds are very powerful tools that, when used in our favor, can make the impossible become possible. We must use these tools to their fullest potential in order to get the most out of our lives.

I will then proceed to discuss our physical health. I believe having a strong and healthy body is of the upmost importance. I do not mean that we all need to be body builders or anything like that. What I do mean is that we must have strong immune systems that are able to function properly and keep us healthy. We should treat our bodies like a temple as we only get one and we spend all our time in them. By being mindful of what we put into our bodies we are able to choose the quality of life we will have.

I like to look at it with the analogy of our bodies being a race car. Life is like the Daytona 500, where we must go through 200 laps to complete, and it is not just a quarter-mile sprint. Are we going to fuel up on premium fuel or on regular? Are we going to get regular maintenance done or are we just going to wait for the engine light to come and then deal with the problems? Are we going to take pit stops to refuel and change our tires or are we just going to push through and eventually run out of gas? We are bound to get further in life if we avoid health problems in the first place.

I will then move on to emotional health. I feel like this is the area that is the least talked about. At least in my world it is. Emotions are taboo for men to talk about, as we have been conditioned to believe that expressing emotion is weak. We do not want to be seen as vulnerable. We are taught to put on a strong face and show no kinks in our armor.

As I have done a lot of work in recent years on my emotional health, I now feel that quite the opposite is true. Showing emotion and vulnerability is a sign of strength and not weakness. Only a real man can stand up in front others and say that he has been hurt. Only a real man can show the scars and declare to the world that although he has been hurt, he is capable of healing and also be willing to forgive. When we give ourselves the freedom to express our emotions, we also give ourselves the freedom to be who we really are.

I will then discuss spiritual health. When I talk about spiritual I do not mean anything religious. To me, spirituality does not include or exclude religion. They can go together for some people and for others they are separate.

To me, spiritual health is about having a practice that helps you be aware of the bigger picture and your place in it. Being aware that there is something out there that is bigger than all of us and is here to support us. Something that connects us all and gives us purpose and passion in life. This is all about finding that connection and letting it guide us in life.

Lastly, I will talk about balance. Balance in life and balance in the four key areas. If we choose to ignore one of the areas, resistance will come up and it will manifest into the other areas. Each area is connected to the others and when there is an issue or ignorance in one area it will show in the others. There is no way to avoid this. This is why balance is so important.

My aim by writing this book is to empower people to make changes in their lives to become healthier and happier. My goal is to help people find meaning, purpose and passion. I want to help people to see they have the tools and knowledge to always move forward in life. Life will always be a series of ups and downs but I want to help you know how to turn the downs into ups. If I can do this, for even one person, then I will have fulfilled my purpose of this book.

Happy reading.

Part 1
Mental Abundance

Chapter 1 - Mindset

"Once your mindset changes, everything on the outside will change along with it."
— *Steve Maraboli*

I believe having the right mindset is the most important thing to do on the road to living a healthy, balanced lifestyle. Mindset includes attitude, willpower, knowledge, motivation and much more. Confucius was right when he said "He who thinks he can and he who thinks he can't are both usually right." What we put into our minds will determine the kind of mindset that we have. Make sure you fill it with information that will push you to grow and move forward in life.

Motivational talks are equivalent to filling your mind with premium fuel. Listening to other people who have been where you are now and how they overcame their struggles will give you the faith and confidence to believe that you can do it too. Autobiographies of successful people are also excellent fuel for your mind. Fill your mind with success stories and things that make you feel good.

Even different forms of entertainment can be considered premium fuel for your mind. Watching documentaries instead of the latest Hollywood flick can be extremely beneficial. Find a topic that interests you and go online to search for documentaries under that category. A lot of documentaries have great producers and directors and are just as entertaining as they are educational. Even by rotating educational and entertainment programs will have an impact on the quality of your mind.

It is important that you fill your mind with positive content that keeps you in a positive mind state. If you are constantly watching the news or "reality t.v" your mind is being programmed for you.. The news is designed to keep you in a state of constant fear and worry. Reality television is designed to have you act and think in certain ways. They teach you how to speak, how to treat others and what is important based on image. These are called television programs for a reason. They are programming your mind to think and behave in a certain way.

It is very important to learn something new every day. This keeps your mind sharp and young. A mind that is constantly working and being challenged is a healthy mind. I believe the quote, "Intellectual growth should commence at birth and cease only at death" by Albert Einstein, sums it up perfectly.

A good place to start is by committing 20 minutes a day to reading. By reading 20 minutes a day, you are exposing yourself to over 3 million words a year and will automatically place yourself in the top 90% of society.

I would recommend reading non-fiction as, in my opinion, they are the most educational books. I love to read about philosophy and history because studying the behavior of humans, the meaning of life and the events of the past can be extremely beneficial. Fiction can also be beneficial as it gets your imagination running. I have definitely learned some valuable lessons from the few fiction books that I have read.

I believe that investing in yourself is the greatest investment that anyone can make and will give the greatest return. If you are constantly looking to become better, smarter, stronger, and more understanding than you were yesterday then you will, by default, also be able to accomplish more than you have ever accomplished before. It can be no other way. This will take time, money, a great deal of effort and commitment but I can guarantee you that it will be worth every second, penny and every drop of sweat.

What does investing in yourself look like? I will give you examples from my own life. Prior to writing this book, in November of 2016, I had spent almost the last four years of my life enrolled in Personal Development classes. These classes have been an investment in many different ways. They have cost me in the thousands of dollars and taken lots of time and energy.

I have also taken other classes outside of the above mentioned. There are many free university classes available online to anyone who wishes to take them. I took classes about public speaking and philosophy. I constantly go to weekend seminars on a variety of topics including motivational seminars. I have also read so many books that I now need to invest in a bookshelf!

In order to make these investments, I have also had to make many sacrifices in my life. I have had to miss soccer games, birthdays, social gatherings, and other kinds of events. I have had to say no to new shoes, phones and even to vacations in order to make sure I had enough funds to keep on investing in myself. Many times I signed up for classes having absolutely no idea how I was going to pay for them but it always worked out one way or the other.

This may seem like a lot to some people and it definitely was a lot for me to handle when I first began this mission of investing in myself. I spent time stressing about money, wondering what I was getting out of it, feeling guilty for missing events and wondering if it was all worth it.

What has been my return on all of these investments and sacrifices? I now have a better understanding of myself and why I am the way that I am. Why I believe in certain things and why I act, feel and think in the ways that I do. I have a better understanding of others and I am able to see things from their point of view and be more empathetic. I have better relationships with the people I care about and most importantly a better relationship with myself.

I have a deeper understanding of the world and my place in it. I know what I can and cannot control. I have learned to forgive and let things go. I have learned about the power of cooperation and how to make a difference in each other's lives and in the world.

I could go on and on about what I have learned and how I have grown and evolved due to investing in myself. I now focus on the benefits of possible investments instead of focusing on the costs.

A lot of people tell me that they want to change yet find it so difficult to do so. The reason it is so easy to keep doing the same things over and over is because it is engrained into your very being since birth. Most of our behaviours, attitudes and beliefs are formed when we are very young and they continue to run the show to this day. We have become very good and efficient at doing what we do. It is like the old saying goes "Practice makes perfect."

Habits can be difficult to break but they can be broken. It takes a good amount of effort, willpower and consistency to do this. Studies have shown that it takes 21 days of practicing a new habit in order to break the old habit and reinforce the new one as the only habit. This is 21 days in a row without skipping days or without doing the old habit at all.

The key here is consistency. There will be challenges and times where you just want to give up and resort back to your old habits. You must use your willpower and think of why you want to change this habit in the first place. Think of the result and how much you will grow from letting go of the old habit. It will take effort on the days where you feel lazy or tired and don't want to push yourself. These are the most important days in which you must really harness your willpower and push through.

Breaking an old habit and replacing it with a new one that will serve you better can be very rewarding. You will have more self-confidence and you will feel a sense of accomplishment that will allow you to move on to the next challenge feeling capable to take it on.

I will give you some simple tips and tools that you can use to successfully break old habits and create new ones that serve you better. Again, I remind you that consistency, willpower and effort will be key to your success.

The first tip is to start simple. I cannot stress this enough. For example, if you want to run 5km every day, but do not currently run now, then it would be best to start with maybe 1km or 2km a day and work your way up. Set yourself up for success. If you try for 5km on the first day and do not make it, it can be very demotivating and likely cause you to give up before you even get going.

Next is the importance of scheduling it into your day. Make sure you schedule time for your run every single day. Do not just say that you will run when you feel like it because that is a recipe for disaster. Slot in the run into your day and do your best to do it at the same time every day. This will help with consistency and it will start to become automatic for you. Scheduling is very important.

Find an accountability buddy and know that it may not be perfect. An accountability buddy is someone that you can share your goal with and that can check in with you and see how it is going. This is important because people often find it easier to let themselves down than letting others down. A buddy will definitely help keep you on track. Also, when challenges do arise, a buddy can provide extra motivation or help talk you through it. Do not expect to be able to change every habit right away but also do not give up. If it takes three tries then it takes three tries. This is where willpower and effort really come in.

Do you know that everyone talks to themselves? Do you also know that the kind of conversations you have with yourself are extremely important? The way you talk to yourself is much more important than anything anyone else could ever say to you.

The way you talk to yourself is so important because you are the one running the show. You decide how you feel, you decide what you do and do not do. You decide what risks to take, if any. You decide what kind of life you are going to live and the friends you are going to have. You decide everything. So if you are always telling yourself that you are ugly or stupid, do you think that might have an effect on the types of decisions you make?

We are very powerful beings who are capable of anything we put our minds to. Therefore, if we believe that we are not capable of something then that stops us from realizing our true power and potential. It is important to always tell yourself you are capable. Even if you do not know how to do something at the moment, you can always learn how to do it.

If you are anything like me, then you most likely spend a lot of time talking to yourself, possibly even more than you talk to others. Make sure these conversations are serving you and helping to motivate you.

Many people will testify to the power of affirmations. "I am" is the most powerful creative tool in existence. Whatever you choose to put after that statement, if repeated enough with faith, will come true. Throughout our lives we have been using this statement for both our support and to our detriment. A lot of what we choose to put after this statement depends on external factors like what people around us tell us. If our teachers keep telling us that we are wrong, we may choose to keep telling ourselves that "I am dumb" and continue to say this throughout life. On the other hand, if one of our coaches tells us that we are an amazingly talented soccer player, we may choose to end that statement with "I am amazing."

Take Muhammad Ali for example. His personal affirmation statement was "I am the greatest!" He told himself this and proclaimed it to the world over and over again. Few would argue against him.

It is important that when you are making affirmations that you root them in the present and prefix them with the "I am" statement. Even if you do not already have what you want, you must still use the present term. For example, if you want to run 5km in under 30 minutes but it currently takes you 35 minutes, your statement could read "I am so grateful to be able to run 5km in 29 minutes." You must root it in the present, attach emotion to it and always begin with "I am".

Another very important aspect of changing your mind and having the right mindset is gratitude. To put it simply, gratitude is just being thankful for what you have. Appreciating where you are at in life and being happy about it.

Gratitude is an emotion that comes from love. Gratitude shows that you have evolved to the point where you are able to choose how you will feel in any given circumstance. Expressing gratitude is able to instantly change your mood into a positive one and has also been shown to lead to better sleep and a stronger immune system.

Expressing gratitude for what you have is important because it shows that material possessions are not what make you happy. If that were the case and you did not express gratitude, then no amount of possessions could ever satisfy your need. This is why so many people in western society are unhappy because we have been conditioned to be consumers and always want the newest phone, or the newest pair of shoes. We are conditioned to compare ourselves to others and value ourselves based on what we own.

One way to start practicing gratitude is by starting a gratitude journal. This can be easy and be done in five minutes or less. At the end of each night, I simply reflect on my day and write down what I was grateful for in that day. It can just be simple point form. This gets you into the habit of focusing on your blessings. Involving other people in your gratitude is a great way to start as well. Share with them what you are thankful for and spread the joy. You can even go as far as telling someone, or writing them a letter that you are grateful for them.

A focused mind is a sharp mind. Like the saying goes "keep your eyes on the prize." It is important to keep free of distractions. Scheduling is also a good way to keep you on track and focused on your goal. By setting blocks of time for certain activities it allows you to be more productive and efficient. When you know you have to work for two hours, then you have recreation time for an hour, then work again for two hours, it gives you motivation and determination to stay on schedule. When you do not have a schedule, it is easy for distractions to put you off track.

A couple of other tips for keeping focused and staying away from distractions is setting restrictions on technology. A lot of people work on computers and the internet is, most likely, the number one distraction of all time. Getting an app that will block certain websites for an allotted time period is an excellent way to make sure you are working and not scrolling through Facebook. Another option is to turn your phone off for certain periods of time. Phones are huge distractions too. 90% of the time when I take my dog out I leave my phone at home or in the car. I want that time to be just ours and free of distractions. Be in the moment. I make our time together meditative.

Decision making is another key trait that successful people have. The reason it is so important to be able to make quick decisions and stick to it is because usually your first thought comes from your intuition and that usually points you in the direction you need to go. It means you trust yourself, you trust your abilities and skills to get the job done. You usually know right away whether or not you are capable of taking on a task and completing it.

Doubt and excuses start to creep in when people take too much time to think about the decision.. The more time it takes to make the decision, the more doubt will get in the way and the less likely you are to do it. Even when the decision is made quickly but then you begin to second guess yourself, it begins to hurt your confidence and self-trust. This will spill into other areas of your life. Doubt is a disease that must not be allowed to spread.

A great example of quick decision making comes from

Napoleon Hill. He is the author of one of the best-selling books of all time called Think and Grow Rich. Andrew Carnegie is the one who set him up for this monumental task of writing that book. When Carnegie presented him with the idea and asked him to make a decision, he was told he had only one minute to decide. Writing the book would require interviewing hundreds of people and take years to complete. Napoleon Hill made the decision in under a minute and the rest is history.

Imagination is another key tool to be able to keep a positive mindset and to be in the right frame of mind. Imagination is so important to success because we need to be able to see the person we want to become before we are there. This allows us to attach emotion to it and to feel what it would feel like to be that person. When we attach emotion to our goals, it becomes real and gives us more motivation to stay focused to make it a reality.

This is why vision boards and visualization exercises have become so popular over the years. When you are able to see something in front of you, it all of a sudden becomes very real. If you do not already have a vision board, I would recommend you make one and put it somewhere that you are going to see it a lot. I also have other small signs around my house. I have a sign that says $100,000 on my bathroom mirror and next to my bed. The more I see, it the more real it gets. I want to keep it constantly in my mind.

This is where the famous Law of Attraction comes into play. The basic premise of the Law of Attraction is that what you focus on will come to you.

This builds on using your imagination and attaching emotion to it as well. Without emotion it is just a nice thought. When you attach emotion it becomes the magnetizing factor that will draw your goal to you. This is why it is the Law of Attraction. You are attracting what it is that you want to you. Our emotions are very magnetic and are always drawing people, experiences, and events to us.

A good way to experiment on this is to practice it with small tasks. One that I like to do is when I am going to the soccer center I will visualize where there will be an open parking spot for me when I arrive. I imagine how great it will feel to not have to walk far and get the spot I want. There are many simple tasks like this that you can do to test it out. Practice makes perfect and the more you use it the better you will get at manifesting what you want from life.

Having fun is another way to make sure you stay in a positive mindset. Having fun is a great way to lighten your load and make your goals be more realistic. When you are being serious all the time and overthinking too much, your tasks start to become heavy and undesirable. When you are having fun, you are full of energy and motivation to keep pushing forward. Keep it simple and make sure fun is involved in all your situations.

Laugh at your mistakes, laugh at yourself. Give yourself the freedom and permission to laugh and enjoy yourself. Work and life do not have to be so serious all the time. Life is meant to be enjoyed and everything starts to flow with ease when you are enjoying it. Time goes by faster and the work seems easier.

Schedule in activities into your life that you love and enjoy. For myself, I have soccer two nights a week and I absolutely love it. If I feel down or angry, I take my dog to the park and just let the emotions go. She is always a blast to spend time with as dogs are the perfect example of what it means to live in the moment. My point is to always make sure, no matter what, to schedule in some fun time in your life.

The last point about mindset is progress. I feel that progress is the ultimate motivator and indicator of where you are at with life.

Everyone loves to check things off that to-do list. Everyone loves to hit that weight goal they had or to hit a new personal best. Everyone loves to score the winning goal or reach the top of a mountain. It makes you feel good and capable of achieving all of your dreams. It gives you confidence and a sense of accomplishment.

Progress shows others and, more importantly yourself, how far you have come and what you are capable of. It shows that you are not just working for nothing and that you are getting somewhere and achieving what you set out to achieve. It is a great indicator of whether or not you are going to be successful.

Setting goals is a great way to monitor progress in life. It is important to set short term and long term goals. People love to know that they are moving closer to their goals. This gives people great confidence and motivation to hit the goals. When one is motivated, it is much harder for distractions to sneak their way in.

It is very important to have a system to track your progress. Be able to check on how you are doing. If you are not hitting your goals then you can make the necessary adjustments to keep pushing forward. If you are hitting your targets then make sure to congratulate yourself or even reward yourself. You earned it and there is no reason why you should not enjoy everything you have accomplished, no matter how big or small.

Chapter 2 – Meditation and Yoga

I mean the whole thing about meditation and yoga is about connecting to the higher part of yourself, and then seeing that every living thing is connected in some way.
– Gillian Anderson

When people think about what meditation is they might picture someone sitting under a tree cross legged or a monk sitting for extended periods of time in a temple. The reality is that this is one method of meditation but there are so many other methods as well. Meditation can take many forms and can be done almost everywhere and at any time that safely allows.

Let's look first at what meditation actually is. Meditation is the art of living in the moment. It is the ability to quiet one's mind and be fully present in the Now. It is being able to focus on one thing and truly experience that event. When you are able to quiet the mind, you allow for inspiration to come in.

Meditation is the ability to go within and find what you are looking for. Society has taught us that all the answers to life's problems lie out there, somewhere waiting to be found. Meditation shows us that actually, quite the opposite is true. It teaches us that everything we need lies within us and that we just need to be willing to listen.

Meditation is trusting yourself and using your own inner power for guidance, confidence, and inspiration. Meditation allows you to tap into an infinite source of energy and wisdom that is here to support you. What you receive from within always comes from a place of love.

There are many reported benefits to making meditation a part of your life. One of the most widely known benefits of meditation is relaxation. When you take the time to quiet the mind it gives your mind a much needed break. Our minds seem to never stop working. Giving your mind some rest can give you extra energy and help you get through the day. People have been known to get more energy by meditating for 15-20 minutes than by taking a nap. Of course, relaxation will also help reduce the stress in your life. Stress is a major factor in causing disease and anything you can do to destress your life should be taken seriously.

Another main benefit of meditation is increased awareness of your own body, of your thoughts, and of the world around you. When the mind becomes silent, you start to notice things you didn't notice before. You can even hear your heart beat and notice how your body reacts to different foods. You can also build an awareness of the different energies around you and feel how they affect your body. Building awareness can help you cope better with the situations you find yourself in.

Meditation is also a great tool to help develop personal growth and a connection to spirit. Once you are aware, you can make a choice on what you want to do about it. If you are not aware of an issue then how could you ever expect to want to fix it? This kind of wisdom and guidance comes from your soul, which is connected to spirit. The word inspiration literally means "in spirit."

I always hear people talk about living in the Now, being present in the moment and things of that nature. What does that really mean though?

To me the "Now" means exactly that, the present moment. For example, if you are peeling potatoes then be fully immersed in the act of peeling potatoes. Feel the peeler in your hand, hear the sounds it makes and feel how the potato feels and looks. Just focus on the act of peeling.

One of the biggest roadblocks to being present in the moment is that people are always thinking of either the past or the future. Worried about what is to come or what has already happened. The past and the future are not real. Yes the past was real when it happened but it does not help to dwell there. The future never comes as every moment we experience is the present. It is important to plan for the future but to worry and stress about it is not beneficial and may hurt your health.

By being totally aware of what you are doing, you get to experience it in a way you never have before and really start to enjoy life. This is one of the reasons I love to play soccer so much. When I am on the soccer field, I don't think of anything else and can say I am truly present in the moment. Being present has the same benefits as meditation and I do consider it to be a type of meditation.

Silence can be a wonderful teacher. Many of us never really experience true silence. "Silence is the language of God, all else is poor translation" – Rumi. I feel like this quote truly exemplifies how wonderful silence can be. If our minds are always full and going 100 mph, how can we ever expect to receive guidance and inspiration? If the mind is full then there is no room for anything else to come in.

When we become silent it allows for all kinds of experiences to come into our lives. You notice smells, sounds, feelings and so much more that you never noticed before. You start to notice how you feel more and think less. This is a benefit because you feel through your heart and think with your brain. Your heart will never lead you astray.

Also, perhaps the best benefit of silence is allowing for inspiration to come in. Inspiration comes from God, from the angels and from spirit. Inspiration can take many forms. It can be anything from a new idea, a feeling, a smell, or even words themselves. You usually receive what you are able to understand and that will benefit you in the moment.

The beautiful part about meditation is that it can literally be done just about anywhere and by anyone. You do not have to be some kind of monk to be able to start meditating. You can start from any level and from the comfort of your own home.

The simplest and, in my opinion, the easiest way to start

meditating is by focusing on your breath. Close your eyes and simply just focus on your breathing. Take long, deep breaths in through the nose and exhale nice and slowly through the mouth. You can do this for as long or as short as you want to. It is said that even just one conscious breath is meditation. Taking deep breaths aids in making sure your blood gets enough oxygen and improves circulation.

Another great way to start meditating is by using guided meditations. Guided meditations are usually pre-recorded and available as mp3 or on YouTube and other forms of online content. They can also be done in person by a facilitator. The wonderful part of guided meditations is that you just need to follow the instructions. Just sit back, close your eyes and let your mind wander. Guided meditations are a great way for beginners to start their practice and explore meditation. In fact, this is exactly how I began my own meditation practice.

Visualization is another great way to begin to meditate. This goes hand in hand with what I talked about earlier when talking about imagination. This can definitely be a type of meditation. Taking time out to visualize or even just to day dream is definitely a meditative activity.

Yoga is an ancient spiritual and ascetic practice. It can be physical, mental, emotional and spiritual all at once.

In my opinion, the purpose of yoga is to gain balance in life. It goes much deeper than just physical balance. It builds harmony between the four key areas of life and helps you move through life with more ease and flexibility. Yoga really begins to show you how each area of life is connected to the others and gives you a better understanding on how we are all connected to one another as well.

I believe yoga is the bridge between the physical, mental, emotional, and spiritual aspects of our lives. It can affect all areas even if you are simply doing it for its physical benefits. The benefits will flow over into the other areas of your life as issues in other areas usually manifest in physical form. By doing the physical work you are also helping to heal the mental, emotional, and spiritual aspects.

When we begin to see this connection our lives begin to change. We realize that what we do mentally affects the physical. We realize that how we feel can have an effect on our spirit and vice versa. We then start to become more conscious of the choices we make as we have a better understanding of how they will affect us on different levels.

When most people think of yoga they simply think of the physical aspects to it. There are indeed plenty of physical benefits to yoga.

Yoga teaches you to harmonize your movements with your breath in order to create ease and relaxation. When you harmonize the two, you use less energy and build balance. You do not have to be flexible to begin doing yoga but flexibility will be a result of practicing yoga. You can just begin at the level you are at. Whether you have ever done yoga before does not matter. There are plenty of beginner classes and tutorials available to get started. Treat it like you would treat a sport, practice makes perfect.

Yoga is also a great way to help prevent injuries or to help recover from an injury. Yoga balances strength with flexibility instead of building strength at the expense of flexibility. Yoga helps to improve your posture. Poor posture is attributed to many physical problems such as back, neck, muscle and joint problems.

The increased flexibility can also help increase your blood flow and get more oxygen to your cells. Moving in and out of poses also drains lymph fluid which helps to boost your immune system. By doing many different poses you begin to move areas of your body that aren't usually moved. This helps to prevent cartilage and joint damage. Yoga also helps to keep the spine healthy by implementing plenty of bends and twists.

There are many mental benefits to practicing yoga as well. Yoga reduces stress and helps to silence the mind as it requires a lot of focus. It is a great way to become present in the moment and build awareness.

Yoga can help reduce reaction times, improve memory and help with problem solving. This can be a result of better focus as your mind begins to empty. Yoga helps to relax your whole system by slowing the breath and shifting our balance from fight or flight to calm and restorative. It is really great to do if you are feeling rushed, overwhelmed or worried. It will definitely help you slow down and find your center.

Many of the mental benefits to yoga are basically the same as meditation. You just come to them in a different manner. I do not feel I need to repeat myself here so I will just say that yoga is definitely a meditative practice and is a good practice to have in a busy schedule as you can work out and meditate at the same time.

Yoga can have an effect on how you feel as well. As I touched on a little earlier, emotional issues usually manifest in physical ways. When you start to heal the physical side it also begins to heal the emotional aspect as well. It will not heal it completely but it is definitely a good place to start.

As you begin to incorporate yoga into your life, you will also begin to feel a better connection to yourself and to others. You will be able to experience different aspects of yourself that maybe you haven't experienced much before. You can have a sense of gratitude, forgiveness, empathy and belonging.

This is where yoga can totally start to become a spiritual practice. As you build a bigger connection to yourself and others and have this sense of belonging you start to see the bigger picture. You begin to see that there is more to the world than just the physical plane. You begin to wonder about your place in the bigger picture and what it is all truly about.

Once you make that connection it is almost impossible to go back to how you were before. It can be life changing and I would recommend to anyone that is serious about reaching their fullest potential to begin to seek out this connection.

Now that you know a lot of the benefits to yoga it is time to start choosing where you will want to practice. There are two obvious choices, at home or at a yoga studio.

First, I would recommend setting aside a few minutes to think about what you want to get out of your yoga practice. Are you doing it just for physical benefits or do you want the mental and spiritual aspects as well? Are you a beginner or do you have experience in other flexible activities such as aerobics? Are you comfortable in groups or prefer being alone? These are some aspects you need to consider before choosing where to practice.

For myself, I prefer to practice at home by myself. I prefer this way as I am after the mental and emotional benefits the most. I like to have my space and quiet time for this. I am easily distracted by others and feel I will get the most mental clarity in silence at home. I also like to have the flexibility of doing it on my own schedule when I can fit it in. I work from home and sometimes when I feel stuck I like to work out, do yoga or go for a walk. Having a home practice makes this perfect for my needs.

I have also been to a gym to do yoga as well. In a group setting, I feel that there is definitely a better chance of having a connection. Feeling connected to those in the space with you and to their emotions and spirit as well. There is something about sharing an experience with others that allows you to connect at a deeper level. Also, when you have an in-person instructor as opposed to an online one, it allows you to connect to them better.

Of course, these are just my own experiences and everyone is different. It is possible to have any kind of experience in each of these settings that you choose. I would recommend trying both settings and finding what feels best for you or even using both in your practice.

One thing I would also like to briefly touch on is that yoga is not just for women. Yoga is definitely for men too. There are plenty of men who practice yoga and will swear by the benefits they have received from their practice.

For years I had wanted to try yoga but I just had a lot of resistance towards it as I felt like it wasn't for men. When I first started doing yoga, one of the first things I realized was that it definitely was not easy. It was more physically demanding than I had ever thought and this also gave me more respect for the strength and determination of women.

Now that I have been doing yoga for almost a year, I do not think about it as being girly and am very open with people about the fact that I do practice yoga. In fact, I now recommend it to a lot of the guys I know when they tell me about aches and pains from working out. It has definitely changed who I am and how comfortable I am in my own skin.

As with any sort of practice, consistency is key. Yoga and meditation are no different. Consistency is important because at the beginning it is always the most difficult to see the benefits. When you keep pushing and become consistent you will find it becomes easier and will start to see results.

The best way to become consistent is to schedule in time for your practice. I would recommend doing yoga at least once a week and meditation once a day. I feel meditation can be done once a day because it can be done during almost any activity. As I said earlier, even peeling potatoes can be mediation if you choose it to be. There are literally a million different ways to meditate and five minutes is more than enough time for a practice.

As you become more consistent in your practice you will find it becomes easier, simpler, and fun. You will look forward to your practice and will begin to do it without needing a reminder.

Part 2
Physical Abundance

Chapter 3 – Food and Water

When diet is wrong medicine is of no use. When diet is correct medicine is of no need.
– Ancient Ayurvedic Proverb

Food and water are two things that we actually need and cannot live without. Making sure your body gets the right quality and amounts of both is vital to your physical health. I like to use the metaphor of your body being a sports car. It is the vehicle you use to navigate through life. It is not just some regular kind of car and should not be treated as such. You want to make sure you are fueling your body with premium fuel and performing regular maintenance.

Let's start off with water. Water is one of the most important elements in existence. Water is necessary for life to be present. Without water there is no life, human or otherwise. It is the most important resource in the world today. Having access to clean, safe water to drink, to bathe and to cook with is of the upmost importance.

There was an author and researcher named Dr. Emoto who thoroughly experimented with water. His main theory was that human feelings, thoughts, and words have an effect on the structure and quality of the water in which they come into contact with. He also said that water has memory, much like humans do. By studying water he could find out what kind of environment it came from, whether it was tap water, rain water, polluted and so much more.

His experiments involved taking pictures of frozen water crystals that had been exposed to different words, music, prayers and pictures to see what effect they would have on the water. The results were quite amazing. Water crystals that were exposed to words like love, happy and gratitude showed beautiful geometric patterns. Water crystals that were exposed to words like hate and anger had crystals that looked like blots of oil spilled. The same results were experienced whether it was music, prayers or other stimulus depending on if it was positive or negative.

This was really ground breaking work being done. Water is such an amazing element that we really do not know much about. I feel like the most important idea we can take away from Dr. Emoto's work is that if our words, thoughts, feelings and actions can have this kind of impact on water, then what are they doing to us? Our bodies are made up of mostly water. What are our thoughts, feelings, words, and actions doing to us? What is the quality of water we are putting into our bodies doing to us?

Dr. Emoto has written several books on the subject and his material is available all over the internet. It is definitely worth investing some time into doing some research on his work to learn about how we can change the quality and molecular structure of the water we are putting into our bodies.

I would now like to talk about the importance of filtering the water you drink to make sure you are getting clean, high quality water in your body.

Tap water, plain and simple, just does not meet the standard for what I consider clean or safe water. When I fill a cup of water from the tap and then fill a cup from my water filter and put them next to each other, the difference is remarkable. Tap water is full of chemicals that are used in the cleaning process and also full of heavy metals that are added into most of North America's water supply. Tap water is exposed to so much pollutants, waste and other harmful substances that to think that the cleaning process would not miss any of this is ludicrous.

When choosing a filter to use for your tap water, it is wise to not just choose a regular filter available at your grocery store. Invest the time necessary to find a filter that will do the best job. Find a filter that is designed to get rid of bacteria and pollutants and that will also get rid of the heavy metals as well. This could involve having two separate filters that make up your main filter. You can find filters on the market that will cost you less than buying a bottle of water per day.

I also do not recommend taking the easy way out and just buying bottled water all the time. There are many reasons for this but I would like to mention two main ones. First, the impact that buying so many bottles and throwing them out has on the environment is insane. This can be avoided by buying a reusable bottle and filling it from your water filter. Second, there have been companies, like Dasani, that have admitted that their bottled water is just tap water. Many bottled water companies also add heavy metals to their water as well, you just need to check the labels and see for yourself. It is hard to tell what you are actually getting from these companies.

It is very important to make sure you are getting the right amount of daily water intake to keep your body performing optimally. Getting the right amount of water can help with digestion and weight loss. Making sure you are always hydrated properly can help you stay healthy and happy.

The most commonly agreed upon amount of water to drink per day is eight 8-ounce glasses of water. That is just under two liters a day. This amount should be increased if you are involved in activities that will make you sweat like sports or the gym. If it is hot outside some extra water would also be recommended to keep you hydrated. Water will help our metabolism and is a calorie free way to quench our thirst. Also, studies have shown that many times when we think we are hungry we are actually just thirsty. Drinking enough water will help us to eat less and aid in maintaining a healthy weight.

There are many risks to your health if you do not get the right amount of water or if you are not hydrated properly. Dehydration warning signs include a dry, sticky mouth, dry eyes, dark urine and vomiting after exercise. Constipation and dizziness are also symptoms that you are dehydrated. Also, the very fact that you are thirsty is the first sign that you may be dehydrated. Dehydration can lead to low blood pressure, rapid heart rate, and can also lead to your organs and cells not functioning as they should.

There are ways to make water more exciting to drink as many people do not like to drink water due to its lack of taste. Adding lemons or lime can add flavor to your water. Even mixing in honey with the lemons has some great health benefits like boosting the immune system and enhancing metabolism. Adding frozen berries to the bottom of your water bottle will allow the berries' flavor to slowly flow into your water over the day. Also many fruits are made up mostly of water. Adding plenty of fruits to your diet will make sure you are getting the necessary amount of water

Moving on to food. I would like to first touch on what foods we should be avoiding and why we should avoid them. There are foods that are high in refined sugars, junk food and all sorts of processed foods that should be avoided when possible. Processed foods are foods that are usually packaged in boxes, cans or bags and can often contain additives, artificial flavoring and other chemicals. These can include products such as MSG and high-fructose corn syrup.

Let's start with why we should avoid foods that have a high amount of refined sugar in the first place. Refined sugars can lead to inflammation, to instable blood sugar levels, and even to diabetes. If you do not exercise regularly, your level of risk of diabetes increases significantly. Refined sugars also affect the PH balance of your body causing it to become more acidic. Disease and bacteria thrive in acidic environments.

There are certain foods that are very high in refined sugar. The most common one is soda beverages. Sodas contain an extremely high level of refined sugar and energy drinks are not far behind either. Even drinks that are labelled fruit drinks can contain a high level of refined sugars too. Do not be fooled just because it says fruit on the label. Usually, the nutritional benefits have been removed from the fruit during the processing and they are nothing more than just fruit flavored sugar water. Chocolate bars, candy and junk food are other sources of refined sugar.

Also, these sugars can often be disguised under different names on the label. Some to watch out for are high-fructose corn syrup and dextrose.

Foods that are high in saturated fat or cooked with oils that are high in fat are also good to avoid. If you cook with oils like vegetable oil, canola oil or corn oil that are very high in fat, consider switching to cooking with coconut oil or avocado oil which are considered as healthy fats. Common high fat foods would be chips, cookies, cakes, fast food and things of that nature. These foods often have no nutritional value at all.

I would like to quickly point out the difference in the kinds of fats. To put it simply, there are two kinds of fats. Saturated fats and unsaturated fats. The good fats are the unsaturated fats. These include poly unsaturated fatty acids and monounsaturated fats. When used in place of saturated fats they can help lower cholesterol and reduce the risk of heart disease. Some examples of good fat sources are avocados, omega 3s and almonds. Saturated fats and trans fatty acids should be eaten less frequent than the good fats. They are found in meats, poultry, dairy and in vegetable fats like palm oils. They can raise cholesterol levels and increase the risk of heart disease.

I want to also mention processed meats and cheese here too. Regular cheese can be healthy but not when it is processed and has had many filler ingredients added to it. It is best to read the label and see if it is real cheese or processed. The same goes for meat. Eating meat can have several benefits when you eat unprocessed meat. Once it has been processed, the risks of having an adverse reaction go up as many additives and preservatives have been added. It is best to do some research and find a local seller who hasn't added additives or preservatives to the meat.

When moving towards adding fruits and vegetables to your diet there is one major issue you need to consider. That issue is the fact that many of our fruits and vegetables are now genetically modified, commonly referred to as GMOs. There are many risks associated with these foods. I believe it is important to avoid these foods.

Like the chemicals and other additives added to our foods, we are told that GMO's are good for us and give us higher crop yields and insect resistant crops. We are not told about the risks that go with them too. Anytime that we start genetically modifying anything we are taking big risks. Whether genetically modifying food, animals or humans, most of the studies done that promote GMOs are done to see how the crop yields perform and to see if it is safe on the environment. If they are found to be safe on the environment then they are deemed to be safe to eat. The problem with a lot of these studies is that the biotech companies that are profiting from GMOs are also the ones paying for the studies to be done. In the U.S. and Canada, no long-term studies have been done to test the safety of eating these foods. However, there are studies in Europe and Russia that have shown GMOs to cause serious health issues to lab mice and rats. In fact, many countries outside of North America have begun banning GMOs altogether. The threat is real and it is best to just avoid these foods until there are some studies done by independent, unbiased parties that show they are safe to eat.

I will say that I do not expect you to just give up all of these foods. Having a cookie here and there will not kill you. Also eating a burger from a fast food chain once a month also will not kill you. I just want to point out how these foods can affect you and that eating them regularly will put you at risk of disease and other conditions. Everything in moderation.

There is also another group of substances that I would like to talk about that we should also do our best to avoid. This group is drugs and alcohol. We as humans do not need chemicals and drugs to be able to live healthy lifestyles.

Our bodies are not meant to intake alcohol and it can have some serious effects when taken regularly. Alcohol is a consciousness altering drug with major side effects. It can severely damage the liver when taken regularly. According to the

Center for Disease Control, long term alcohol use can lead to high blood pressure, heart and liver disease and even stroke. They say it can also lead to various types of cancer, learning problems, mental health problems and social problems. They said that during the years of 2006-2010 that excessive alcohol use led to 88,000 deaths in the United States (U.S.) and has shortened the lives of those people by 30 years!

Drugs are another substance that can have some serious side effects and can lead to death. When I mention drugs, I am talking about prescription drugs just as much as street drugs like heroin. However, I am not talking about any plants as I do not consider plants to be drugs. All drugs have side effects, whether they are street drugs, over the counter drugs or prescription drugs. Sometimes the legal drugs, that we are told are safe and are offered to us since our youth, are the most dangerous ones. It is best to do some serious research before making the decision to take any form of drugs. Research the risks involved and decide if you are willing to take that chance.

Often these chemicals that are added to our food supply have more risks than potential benefits to our health. We usually are not told about the risks and are only told about the potential of benefits. We are told that certain chemicals will help keep our crops safe from insects, or will help them yield larger harvests but are not told the cost it will put on our health.

Then when we do get sick, we are always told to take some kind of drug to get better. I find it crazy that when you do see drug commercials, that in small print or at the end they tell you this may also cause this list of issues and should not be taken by anyone that has this list of issues. There is a great risk anytime we choose to use these drugs and I do not believe drugs should always be our first resort when something is wrong.

I want to mention that just like the foods I mentioned to avoid above, the consumption of these substances from time to time is not going to kill you. When I say that we should avoid these substances I mean avoid having them be a part of your regular diet. Having a few beers every day will catch up to you and have adverse effects. The thing with a lot of these substances is that the effects will not be seen until you are older and the damage has already been done.

I do believe drugs do have a time and place when it comes to health. It would also be crazy to say that drugs have zero benefit to them. I feel people should be educated on other alternatives as well and be able to make an informed decision on the matter. If we, as a society, truly want to start being healthier we need to educate ourselves and make informed decisions.

There are plenty of medicines that are available on the market today that are 100% natural. I recommend using these as you will not be putting anything harmful into your body and they are absorbed easier by your body as well. Even picking alternatives to traditional medicine is suggested as well. For example, by using honey and ginger to soothe a sore throat instead of taking over the counter drugs. Simple changes like this to your lifestyle can have a big impact on your health and your life.

There are some alternatives we can begin to use in place of some of these unhealthy foods that have become such a staple in our diets. These are simple choices that can have a great benefit to our health.

Choosing to use pink Himalayan salt instead of white salt can have a positive effect and your health. Regular table salt has added chemicals to it and Himalayan pink salt does not. As with anything, the more natural a product the better for your health. Himalayan pink salt is over 200 million years old and contains 84 minerals that are more easily absorbed by our bodies than regular salt. This can help to boost our immune system, help with skin conditions and help detox our skin and organs.

As I mentioned before, some of the oils we may cook with are not the best choice for cooking as they are full of bad fats. Switching over to coconut oil or avocado oil is much healthier choice as they are full of good fats. There are also numerous benefits to having coconut oil be a regular part of your diet. It can provide you energy for the day, can prevent heart disease and high blood pressure and reduces inflammation. It is worth looking into and making a part of your diet.

Another change you can make is choosing where you get your sugar from. I have already talked about how refined sugars are bad for you. Fruits and vegetables are a great source for naturally occurring sugar. If you need to have sugar as a part of your diet, fruits and vegetables are definitely the way to go. Most fruits do contain a good amount of natural sugar in them and it is worth looking into which ones provide what amount.

Eating less meat can have numerous advantages. I am in no way saying that we should cut meat completely out of our diets. I am just saying that we definitely do not need to eat meat in every meal or even every day.

Eating meat is very taxing on our digestive system and makes our organs work harder. Our digestive system needs to use a high amount of acids to digest meat and our body then needs to use our calcium reserves to neutralize these acids. Having a high meat diet can lead to calcium deficiency and other issues. Calcium is needed to stabilize blood pressure and build strong bones and teeth. It is best to eat meat with a high fiber content like raw salads or steamed vegetables.

There are several benefits for choosing to not eat meat for even just one day. It gives your body a break by allowing the digestive system and organs to not work so hard. This will lead to increased energy and feelings. By not eating meat, you will be eating meals that have more fiber than protein which will help cleanse the intestinal walls and digestive system. You will still get the necessary protein for your diet from other foods.

There are also huge benefits to the environment and world around us that are worth considering as well. According to recent studies, if everyone in the world did not eat meat one day a week, over one billion animals would not need to be factory farmed!! That is a huge difference in the world. One billion animals would not need to be slaughtered. Factory farming is one of the biggest pollutants to the environment. It takes a lot of resources to run these farms, transport the meat and process. If people replaced chicken from one meal a week it would be the equivalent of taking 500 000 cars off the road. The U.S. alone would save 100 million gallons of water if everyone didn't eat meat for one day. 1.5 billion pounds of crops that would feed those animals could go towards feeding humans that do not have food.

The benefits to the world and environment are astronomical and I could literally go on all day on this topic. My point is not that we need to stop eating meat completely. The point here is that we need to make more conscious choices about what we eat and about what consequences come from those choices. What kind of impact do we want to have on our world? Would not eating meat for just one day really be that difficult? I think anyone can do it and it would be quite the challenge and fun to try out new dishes and recipes.

Nature is the best source of nutrition and medicine available and also provides us absolutely everything that we need to not only survive, but to thrive and live rich, healthy lives. There are a lot of medicines and health supplements that are made from the plants that inhabit the Earth. Fruits and vegetables are the best and most natural source we have to get our needed amount of vitamins and nutrition. It is important that we make sure we get enough of both in our diet so that we stay healthy and prevent disease. There are also plenty of medicines available that are 100% natural and do not contain chemicals in them.

Many fruits and vegetables have antioxidants and anti-inflammatories inside which help prevent and eliminate colds, flus and other sicknesses. Fruits and vegetables help with digestion, blood pressure, weight maintenance, cleansing, energy, eyes, heart and teeth. There is literally no part of your body that a fruit or vegetable cannot help you with.

Choosing to buy organic fruits and vegetables is the best way to go. This is the way nature intended us to have our foods. It is hard to imagine that we, as humans, could make something better than nature can. If we have the right diet consisting of plenty of organic fruits and vegetables, we will have a very good start to living a healthy lifestyle.

Buying organic also has other impacts on our lives as well. When we consciously choose where we will spend our hard earned money we are showing these large corporations, like Monsanto, what we stand for. GMO corporations either need to change their practices or they will not receive our money. I believe that voting with our dollars is more effective than voting at the polls. People notice when their wallets are hurt, more than they notice a protest or who you vote for. Another huge factor is that you are supporting organic farmers. Organic farms are generally smaller businesses and not huge multi-national corporations. Buying from organic farmers shows our support for what they produce and how they do it. This gives them hope and motivation to keep moving forward.

Growing your own food can be one of the most rewarding things you can do. You know exactly what you are getting and choose the quality. You can save a lot of money and perhaps even make some while you are at it. It may sound odd at first too but, growing your own food is the most revolutionary thing you can do.

When you grow your own food you do not have to worry about whether or not your food has been sprayed with chemicals, whether it has been handled properly or any of that other stuff that you worry about when buying from the store. You buy the seeds, you grow and nurture it and you get to enjoy it afterwards. Something you are giving life to is also giving life to you. It is a beautiful process to be a part of and I believe everyone should grow at least one food for themselves.

By growing your own food you will save money by not having to buy what you grow. It may not be enough to get you to retire but every dollar counts. If you grow more than you need for yourself you can even sell some of it or trade people for what they have too much of. There are plenty of options at your disposal when you begin to grow your own food. Also spending time outside and with plants can be rewarding in of itself.

There is another section of food that I feel I need to mention to make this chapter whole and to give you an edge on getting healthy. This section is for superfoods. You may or may not have heard of them but they are becoming very popular and for good reason.

Superfoods are pretty much the natural equivalent to supplements. They are nutrient rich foods that can greatly benefit your health if you incorporate them into your diet. Some fruits and vegetables certainly do fall into this category and also some fish and dairy too. The main point I want to get across is that these foods are nutritionally dense and that getting the right amount of nutrients from a variety of foods is the most important. We cannot get everything from just eating bananas for example. We need variety.

Most dark leafy greens are considered superfoods. Plants like kale and spinach are very good for your health. Broccoli and lentils are two other great examples. There are also berries such as blueberries and strawberries that are very nutritious. There are many seeds like chia, quinoa and hemp seeds that have great health benefits too. Almonds and pistachios are another great source. My point here is that finding what these nutrient dense foods are and what their benefits are can be a great step in the right direction.

There are also natural powders that are very nutritious and can be added to your diet easily. Foods like spirulina and triphala that are rich in nutrients and health benefits. Turmeric has an endless list of benefits to it. Psyllium husk can be a great benefit to your digestive health. Coconut oil is one of my favorites for sure. Like turmeric, it has a huge list of benefits and can literally be used for almost anything.

There are certain times of the day that are optimal for having your meals. Breakfast is important because it gets your day going and by having a healthy breakfast you give your body the proper nutrition to get through the day. You were just sleeping for eight hours and your body needs to refuel. If you do not eat breakfast you can start to feel fatigued, cranky, and overly hungry. I always eat breakfast soon after waking up and never leave the house without eating. I usually start my day with a smoothie made up of a mix of fruits and greens. I can get most of my daily nutritional needs met with the proper mix of fruits and vegetables in this one meal.

Lunch should be eaten four to five hours after you eat breakfast. You want to make sure to get this meal in to enable you to finish your work day with enough energy and motivation to be productive. If you work away from home, you do not want to skip lunch as going eight or more hours without a proper meal is not healthy and can cause problems for your body.

Dinner should be eaten about four to five hours after you eat lunch. Dinner can be lower in calories as people tend to be less active at night time than they are during the day. You do not want to skip dinner as it would be a very long time before breakfast comes around the next day.

It is also beneficial to have snacks in between meals and to get enough water. Having healthy snacks like bananas or apples and other fruits can give you the needed energy and nutrients to feel good until the next meal.

This brings me to one of my favorite parts about having a healthy diet. As I have mentioned a few times already, I love to start my day with a smoothie. Smoothies are easy and convenient to make. They are a great way to make sure you are getting all the nutrients you need for your day. They are also a lot of fun as the variety is pretty much limited only by your imagination.

It does not take much time at all to make a smoothie. All you need is a blender and a knife and cutting board depending on what you are adding. Making it, drinking it and cleaning up after can all be done in 15 minutes. If you are anything like me and take your time getting up in the morning, this is a great way to get a really nutritious breakfast without lots of effort.

Smoothies are the perfect way to make sure you get everything you need. I make sure there are fruits and vegetables in every smoothie I have so I get the right mix of nutrients. I also always add hemp seeds to make sure I get the right amount of protein in my diet. I usually add honey, apple cider vinegar and coconut oil as having all three in your diet have numerous benefits. I usually add a powder like spirulina or triphala for an extra boost of health too.

Each smoothie I make is different and keeps my taste buds excited. The combinations are endless and worth exploring. Experimenting with different combos to see which taste better, give you more energy, help you hydrate for sports or whichever benefit you are looking for, can be fun and rewarding. Sharing smoothie recipes with friends and family can be lots of fun as well.

This chapter will conclude with the importance of cleansing. Cleansing helps to remove harmful toxins and other harmful build up from your body. Cleansing gives your organs a break from working so hard all the time. Cleansing also makes you feel better and gives you more energy. Everyone should make cleansing a part of their routine especially if you have never done one.

Cleansing can help eliminate toxins and other waste in our bodies. Our bodies carry around 5-10 lbs of built up waste. That is actually very disgusting if you think about it. Being able to flush that out will improve your digestion, give you clarity, energy and so much more. There are different types of cleanses you can do but the best for getting rid of this waste is colon hydrotherapy. Colon hydrotherapy is like a bath but for the inside of your colon. Filtered, temperature regulated water flows into the colon to help soften and loosen the accumulated waste. It is best to see a professional hydro-therapist to have this done. On top of helping digestion and elimination of toxins it will help your body reset and perform the way it is supposed to. The colon is the best place to start when thinking of what kind of cleanse to do as it is the body's sewage system and an important part of keeping your body healthy.

Most cleanses involve having a lot of fruits and vegetables and little to no meat. A lot of them are based around juicing and smoothies and also raw foods. This helps give your organs a much needed break as they do not have to work as hard to digest raw foods. Our digestive system and organs work around the clock to digest meats and cooked food. It is best to give them a break from time to time to keep them performing optimally.

Cleansing your body can have great effects on your mind as well as your body too. You will feel lighter, have more energy and be more confident. I can say this as I have done cleanses and have felt great afterwards. I feel clean, healthy and motivated. Knowing that I gave my body a break and got rid of toxins and waste is a great feeling. If you start to eat right and cleanse regularly the cravings for junk will start to go away. You will notice what eating properly does to your body and will only want to feel that way.

By making sure that you are only feeding your body with high quality, natural food and water you are giving yourself the best chance to be healthy. Staying away from junk and using natural alternatives instead of drugs will also make a big difference. Then, making sure to do regular cleansing will keep you in peak condition.

Chapter 4 – Exercise

To enjoy the glow of good health you must exercise.
Gene Tunney

Exercise is a very important element to living a balanced, healthy lifestyle. I think it is unheard of to find someone who is healthy that does not exercise. Our bodies are built to move and to be active. If we do not use them in this way we are not going to live to our fullest potential. Our bodies will become static and rusty similar to a car that has been parked all winter; it will need a tune up, oil change and other maintenance before being brought out for the summer.

Our bodies need to move and want to move. They want us to use them physically and push them to grow and be stronger. The more we exercise the more muscle we build, the younger we will feel and the more energy we will have. The fresher our bodies are, the easier it is to stay healthy too. It is easier to stay healthy mentally and emotionally when we have strong physical bodies as well.

There are a significant amount of benefits to making exercise a part of your daily routine. There are benefits to our mental and emotional health on top of the physical benefits. To add to that list, there are also benefits to the quality of our lives and to our long term health as well.

I like to use the term weight management instead of weight loss for a few reasons. Firstly, weight loss is not the only thing people are doing to want to stay healthy. Some people want to gain weight and some people just want to stay where they are at without gaining or losing weight.

I believe that whether your goal is to lose weight, gain weight or to stay the same weight, that exercise needs to be a regular part of your routine. You would be doing different kinds of exercise for each different case but would be an equally important part of your routine.

Exercise can help you burn fat, build muscle and feel better almost instantaneously. Well, at least, the feel better part, the fat burning and muscle building will be more gradual and take more time and effort. Exercise can help you feel more confident, capable and just plain happier.

I want to expand on what happens to our bodies if we do not use them physically on a regular basis. For a large percentage of the population our jobs require us to either sit or stand for extended periods of time. We do not get to move around much or to stretch and take care of our bodies. On average an American adult spends 8-10 hours a day sitting! This is so much sedentary time that even if you work out for 30-60 minutes a day it will not counteract the hours of just sitting around. This can have some serious effects on your health.

Some other risks of being sedentary for long periods of time are slower blood circulation and your muscles will also burn less fat. Sitting after you eat can lead to digestion problems which can then lead to several other health problems. Being sedentary has been shown to lead to different types of cancer including colon cancer. When we move around, our bodies create anti-oxidants that fight cancer causing free-radicals. Also, the associated weight gain and other side effects of being sedentary are factors for the cancer as well.

Do your best to not be sedentary for extended periods of time. Even by taking five to ten minutes every couple hours to stretch or go for a walk to a co-workers desk or walking to the store instead of driving can improve your health and lower the risks of disease. I will give tips on how to easily add exercise into your daily routine later in this chapter.

Should you be working out at home or at the gym? Working out at home can be extremely convenient and easier to fit into your schedule. You have a great variety of different workouts you can do at home as long as you have a good size space. There are many free online tutorials which can help. You can save money by choosing to work out from home as you will not have membership fees to pay or gas to use. You can work out free of distractions and then just jump in your shower and be clean, fresh and ready for your next activity. Some cons of at home training can be lack of equipment, space, motivation and in some cases more distractions. The couch can look so appealing when you do not feel like working out.

The gym has the convenience of having everything you need in one place. The gym I go to has a lot of options in the facility. There is a running track, pool, hot tub, steam room, showers, weights, cardio equipment and gyms. I meet friends there sometimes and we push each other to go harder. Some of the cons are that they can get quite busy sometimes and you may have to wait to use equipment, sometimes not everything is in working condition, you have to pay, and of course travel time and gas.

There are other options like running outside which I love to do with my dog as she makes the perfect running partner. I go to the dog park or for walks almost every day and sometimes even twice a day. Going for a bike ride, to the waterpark, rock climbing and so many more activities can be found. The options are limitless.

Team sports is also a great way to get active and a great way to be social at the same time. I absolutely love the atmosphere that team sports provide. It is a chance to see my friends that I wouldn't otherwise get to see. We practice together, we work hard together and we win and lose together. It is hard to describe in words the kind of relationship that is formed on a team that works hard and plays hard. Truly one of my favorite things to do and I have so much fun doing it. It definitely adds years to my life and helps keep me young at heart.

You also get to learn a lot about yourself and how you handle group dynamics. Team sports is the perfect opportunity to test out your leadership skills or how you are able to support others. It is the perfect place to provide a mirror for the rest of your life.

Do you go to practice? Do you show up on time? Do you hustle hard and support your teammates? Do you get angry when you lose? I am a firm believer in the idea that how you do one thing is how you do everything. By analyzing how you show up for the team, you get the opportunity to see how you show up in all areas of your life.

Team sports are also a great way to stay motivated and get that extra boost of desire to get out of your house and be active. Knowing that your team depends on you to show up is a great motivational factor. The fact that you will get to see your friends and hang out with them afterwards is a great boost as well. You can bring your family and other loved ones to watch and is truly an event that you can involve your whole circle in. Also, we are less likely to not show up to team sports as opposed to when it is just going to the gym as we would rather let ourselves down than let others down.

I feel like one of the biggest obstacles to people being active is time. I want to give you some tips on how to start being active on a busy schedule.

There are simple changes you can make to be more active in your life. You can take the stairs instead of the elevator. You can park farther away than you usually would and walk the extra bit. Walk to the store or ride your bike. In the spring and summer I love riding my bike to the gym and even ride it to soccer practice sometimes. My mom loves to work out while watching television. She will lift weights or other activities while watching her favorite shows and even go up and down the stairs during commercials. She takes the train to work and walks to the train station every day instead of driving or taking the bus. Little changes like these add up and can make a big difference to your health.

As you can see by the above examples, getting active does not have to be super time consuming. Especially when you start to mix activities together. Do you want to exercise and meditate but feel like you only have time for one? Then do yoga. It is the perfect activity where you can meditate and be active at the same time. Meditate in the shower after working out. When you say yes to exercise you will find the time. You get the chance to be creative in finding ways to combine activities or make changes to your lifestyle to allow you to be more active. Just the process of creativity and change can be a reward in of itself.

I believe that if you do want to lose weight, eating healthy will not be enough. Exercise needs to be a part of your plan as well. You need to burn calories and get your body moving. Exercise helps get the heart pumping and the blood flowing. One good tip is to go for a walk after having dinner or other meal. It will help settle the food you just ate and help burn the calories as well. Depending on the amount of weight you want to lose you will need to exercise almost daily. This does not have to be hard. It can be as simple as a 20 minute jog, 30 minutes of yoga or a quick trip to the gym.

For people that want to gain weight it is important to eat enough to fuel your body for the workouts you will require. A lot of people that want to gain weight want to gain muscle. Muscle building exercises require a lot of energy and you want to make sure you are giving your body the right fuel it needs. Once you do start eating more to fuel your body, you will want to make sure you do not miss your planned exercises or that extra intake of food will start to turn to extra pounds of fat instead of muscle.

Even for people that just want to maintain their current weight it is important to get regular exercise. I am one of the people that just wants to maintain my weight. I have seen how easy it is to have a couple bad meals and miss a couple workouts and all of a sudden you have gained five pounds. It happens so fast that it is almost unbelievable. It is much harder to lose that extra five pounds that it was to gain it. That is why it is so important to avoid the situation in the first place and just make sure you get active daily.

These are all great examples of how regular exercise can help you get fit and stay fit. To be fit you must exercise. There is no shortcuts or other way around it. I feel that once it is a part of your regular routine that you will love it and look forward to your next chance to flex your muscles.

One of the greatest motivations for people to get active is wanting to look and feel better. Looking better to me is such a broad and general term. Looks are all based on perspective and beauty lies in the eyes of the beholder. What one person finds to be beautiful another can find to be ugly. We really should only use our perception of our beauty as a measuring pole to how we feel about ourselves. As we move closer to our weight goals we will start to look better to ourselves. Whether we are wanting to lose or gain weight, when we notice the difference we will look better. This will help keep us motivated to keep pushing forward.

Exercise can also makes us feel better. This is proven by science and lots of research in this area. Our body releases endorphins when we exercise that makes us feel happy and joyous. Also, exercise helps us to focus on the task at hand and clear our heads. It helps us live in the moment and not worry about anything else. I have had days that were rough and I felt like crap but then I went to soccer. After being on the soccer field and running around I felt like a totally different person afterwards and was able to move forward with a new perspective on my problems. Exercise truly is more than just physical.

Consistency is the key to getting these results. Especially for physical changes. Your body is definitely not going to look any different after one session at the gym. You can feel better after one session but if you want to feel better all the time then you definitely need to exercise regularly. I find that on the days that you feel unmotivated to do your workout, but exercise anyways, will be the most rewarding days. You dug down deep and kept your agreement to yourself. You showed great commitment and willingness to be better. These are the days that you will feel like a million dollars and these are the days that will create a new character for yourself. These are the days that you will look back on when you reach your goals and be thankful that you pushed through. These are the days that will keep you consistent and on track.

I have also found that by being active you actually have an abundance of energy instead of having less energy. Studies have shown that exercise is a great way to fight fatigue. In fact, it has also been shown that taking a walk instead of taking a nap can leave you feeling more energized. Studies have also shown that exercise is a much better stimulant than any energy drink or coffee can be. Also, the best time to exercise is in the morning. It will provide you with that extra spark of energy you need to make it through the day. If you do not believe me just give it a try and trust the results. Also, do not forget to give your body the proper fuel before and after each workout.

There have also been many studies shown that doing the opposite of exercise, such as sitting around doing nothing, drains your energy. Oversleeping can be a cause of fatigue. Our bodies have mechanisms that tell our cells when it is morning and they begin to use their energy whether we are awake or not. I have heard being sedentary be referred to as the "sitting disease." This is because it is such a drain on your energy and health. Usually when people are being sedentary they are watching television or other like programs which have a negative effect on our systems. It puts us into different brain wave cycles which decrease our energy. The less time we spend being sedentary the better our energy levels will be.

Exercising in the morning can be very beneficial. What better way to feel awake and alive and ready to take on the world than by having a workout and getting your heart pumping and blood flowing. A morning workout will wake up all parts of your body including your spirit and mind. It will have you alert and aware and ready for what is to come.

Going to the gym, soccer field or the pool or whatever you choose is also the perfect way to get your mind off things. Releasing some frustration and anger or any other feelings while you exercise is a great way to feel better. It allows you to let go of your issues even if just momentarily. When you come back to the problems after, you will have a fresh mind and clearer perspective which often helps you find more creative solutions that you could not think of when you were stuck feeling stressed and frustrated.

Exercise plays another important role in our lives too. Exercise can help us deal with our fears. Fear can be mental, physical, and emotional too. I feel like it can be completely conquered in the physical. Mental and emotional fear manifests in the physical by paralyzing us and causing us to not take action. When we get that strange feeling in our gut or heart and we just stay home or avoid situations, that is fear acting out in the physical. The best way to beat this feeling is by taking action. Feel the fear and do it anyways. The more and more you do what you are scared of, the less you will feel the fear. The things you were once afraid of will begin to be a part of your comfort zone.

A body that is strong and healthy is less likely to feel fear. It is less likely to be paralyzed out of fear and less likely to be inactive. You need to be active to have a strong, healthy body in the first place. A body that is strong will be able to overcome the physical sensations easier and with less hesitation. A strong mind will know that on the other side of fear lies success. Taking care of your body properly is the first step to take if you want to put fear out of your life.

Exercise will also help you grow as a person. If you are able to develop a consistent, strong routine and excel at it then this will spill over into other areas of your life too. By making your body strong and healthy you also grow your mind, spirit and emotional health. They are all linked and by working on one you help the others grow too.

Exercise will help you to gain certain qualities that are required to be successful. By reaching your exercise goals you gain confidence in your abilities. Confidence is key to any endeavor you choose to set out on. It is rare for someone who lacks confidence to succeed and to keep that success. Determination, perseverance and hard work are other qualities you will possess. There are so many character traits that are developed by getting physical and in shape.

Exercise is also a great way to get meditative and live in the moment. It is a great time to focus and be free of distractions. I use exercise as a meditative practice to have more harmony in my movements.

I feel that most kinds of exercise require your full attention. Depending on what you are doing it could be dangerous if you are not giving your full attention to the task at hand. For example, you cannot be doing the bench press and texting at the same time. That could have some disastrous results. It is the perfect time to practice focusing on the task at hand and clearing your mind of distractions. The more you focus, the more at ease your mind will be. With a stronger body and calmer mind you will be able to achieve more in your life.

I use my love of soccer as a time to also practice meditation. I am very conscious of the way I breathe when I am on the field. I want to get the most energy and oxygen to my body so that I can perform at my best. Focusing on breathing is one of the best ways to begin to meditate. It helps me calm down and relax which helps me tremendously as I put a lot of pressure on myself to perform at a high level. This helps me in other areas of my life when I feel pressured as I think what I would do if I were on the soccer field right now. It has definitely helped me get more in touch with my inner self.

Your quality of life will definitely take a turn for the better when you make a conscious choice to make exercise a part of your life. I mentioned how it makes you feel and look better. The confidence and other character traits that you will develop will help you overcome many obstacles beyond just the physical ones. You will be happier and other people will notice this too. They will most likely notice that before they notice the physical changes you have went through. Energy speaks louder than words and images ever will.

You will lead a healthier life and also live longer. I don't feel like I need to say this but will mention it anyways. Having a strong, healthy body will allow you to live longer. Everything you gain from exercise will help you to live longer. Being happy and confident will help you to live longer. Eating right and growing as a person will help you to live longer. Taking care of your body and exercising regularly will improve your life and prolong your life in so many ways. It is definitely worth the time investment because it is one of the only investments that will earn you more time to spend doing the things you love!

Part 3
Emotional Abundance

Chapter 5 – Emotional I.Q

"There is within the human heart a quality of intelligence which has been known to surpass that attributed to the human mind."
Aberjhani

It is time to talk about our emotions. This is a very difficult subject for me to write about as for most of my life I have kept people from getting close to me so that I would not have to talk about my emotions. Growing up I never talked about my emotions with anyone and for the most part that has carried into my adult life. Only until the last few years in which I have been enrolled in personal development classes have I started to open up about how I feel and how I have felt in the past.

I feel that many people can relate to my story of not talking about how they feel. It is looked down upon in today's society to show emotion as it is perceived as being weak. I feel that all of our emotions come from two root emotions. Those emotions are love and fear. I truly do believe that all other emotions are just side effects of these two.

Why is it that society is built to keep us from showing too much emotion? It seems like society only wants to know when you are happy but if you are not happy you should keep it to yourself or you will be ridiculed, seen as weak or prescribed some drugs for your condition. I remember in elementary I was teased some times for different reasons and there were some times I cried at school. As a result, I was teased some more and viewed differently by the other kids. It was at this point where I decided that I would just do my best to keep my emotions inside and not show them to others. I feel that especially for men, society has made it the norm to keep our emotions bottled up inside.

This, to me, is where a lot of the fear emotion comes into play. My own example about keeping emotions bottled up is the perfect example of other emotions coming from fear. I was scared I would be teased, laughed at, beat up or other things if I showed emotion. I began to get angry, lonely, and sad. All of which stemmed from my fear. Fear manifests in many different ways and leads us to act out in ways which we would not normally behave. As a result of this behavior we will feel other emotions that are just by-products of fear.

Love works in much the same way as fear does but in a positive manner rather than a negative one. When you are shown love and you also show love, you are opened up to a whole other range of emotions. When you play with your friends or your siblings, you are exposed to fun, joy, excitement and pleasure. My love of soccer is the perfect example of this. Through that love I have been opened to excitement, adrenaline, wonder, enjoyment, and brotherhood with my teammates. Much of the same emotions come from the love I share with my family and friends. Love opens us up to a much wider range of emotions than fear does and it feels so much better too. Love is growth and expansion, while fear is controlling and inhibiting.

I feel that fear is more based on the ego and aligned with the brain while love is more aligned with the heart. It has been scientifically proven that the heart is actually more powerful than the brain. Love is also the most powerful emotion in existence and fear pales in comparison to this.

There is an institute that is solely dedicated to doing research on the power of the heart. They are called the Heart Math Institute. They have proven that the heart is literally thousands of times more powerful than the brain both electrically and magnetically. This is why it is so important to use emotion with your affirmations because your heart is very powerful at attracting what it wants. They have also proven that our hearts are sending more signals to our brain than our brains send to our heart. The heart is literally running the show. The heart is also the first organ to develop in our bodies and runs the show from the very beginning.

There is no comparison to the power of love. When we act

out of a place of love we can literally accomplish anything we want. When people work together for a common goal, mountains can move. When we act with love we act in harmony with everything around us. This creates synergy and we all know it is easier to accomplish goals together than alone. Fear keeps us divided and mistrusting of each other. Fear keeps us alone and causes us to self-sabotage our own projects and those of others. I feel like the quote by Jimi Hendrix sums it up the best, "When the power of love overcomes the love of power the world will know peace." There is so much truth behind those words.

I feel that we need to consciously make the decision on what we are going to act out of. Fear or love? When we automatically react to events or people, we need to take a step back and ask ourselves which emotion is driving this reaction. We need to become more aware so that we are able to change the world around us. All of us have automatic reactions that are triggered by certain events. The more conscious we are of these triggers, the sooner we can make a change and choose to react out of love instead of fear.

Now that I have explained that all actions are based on either love or fear I would like to talk about events. More specifically, I would like to say that all events are neutral. Meaning that they are neither good or bad, right or wrong. How could events be anything but neutral? They do not have feelings, they do not choose who they happen to and they have no motives. Events just happen and we are the ones who choose how to react to them. It is up to us how we will react and how we will feel.

Our perceptions and our past experiences are what we use to determine how we judge the event to be. Our belief system also plays a big role in our judgement. For example, if we have a belief that we must follow all rules no matter what, then we may think there is something horribly wrong with someone jaywalking when there is no one around for miles. When inherently, there is nothing morally wrong with this event at all. No one is being harmed and nobody has been affected in any way.

This is how 10 different people can go to the same party and all have different experiences. One person might say it was the best night of her life, while another person says it was horrible and the music was too loud. Another person might say it wasn't the right crowd and another might say they made so many friends and met some awesome people. Our belief system is once again at work here. We each have a different belief on what makes for a good party and what kind of people we like to be around.

In the same way that events are neutral I also believe that words are neutral as well. Words in themselves do not have the power to hurt anyone either. Depending on who says the words and in the way they are said we feel offended or not. Again, it is our beliefs and perceptions that decide whether we allow words to hurt us or not.

Words, just like events, have no feelings or motives. Almost every word has multiple meanings and can be used in a wide variety of ways and in different context.

One of our friends could make a joke about one of our features and we would be fine with it. Yet when a stranger or someone we don't like says the same thing we could get offended and become triggered to feel a certain way.

It is our perception of the word and who is saying it that triggers us again. Our belief system comes into play here again. Maybe we have a belief that it is ok for a friend to say something but not for a stranger. There's a line some people can cross with their words and others cannot. Here, just like in every situation, the choice is ours in whether we choose to feel offended or just move on.

We have a choice to make in every situation. That choice is how we will choose to perceive people, events and other situations and how we will react and feel. This is very much a choice that we get to make and it is important to realize that we do have this power.

It is hard to grasp the idea that we do indeed have this choice to make. It is because most of us have just been running on auto-pilot for our whole lives. We just react to what happens and never take a step back to ask why am I reacting like this and is it serving me and those I am interacting with. When we can take the step back and just observe, we will start to notice our triggers and the automatic reactions. We then get to make a conscious choice as to whether or not that is how we want to react.

Choosing how to feel can be a little bit trickier but we do still get to make this decision. They key in choosing how to feel about any given situation is first choosing how you perceive that situation to begin with. For example, I would always get angry when guys on my soccer team showed up late or didn't show up at all. This would carry over into the game or practice and would affect the way I would play. Now when it happens I choose to look at it different. I say ok well who do we have here and what are our options. What can we do with the guys here and let's make sure we have a plan for the guys that are here. I have accepted that I cannot control who shows up and have decided to just focus on working with what I have. This way I get to feel focused, calm, controlled and on purpose.

If I do not reframe the story and just try to feel differently I would have a much harder time. I would still be focused on the fact that people are late or not there and be triggered by my beliefs about what it means when people are late. The choice to feel different is much easier when I choose to reframe the story. When I choose to look at the situation differently I then start to feel different too.

It is important for us to understand and accept that there truly is a choice in every situation. Life starts to flow much smoother and calmer when we can step back and make conscious choices instead of just being triggered and reacting automatically. If you ever do find yourself feeling triggered, just take a step back for a minute and play the role of the observer. It will go a long way in allowing you to choose how to feel.

There are some simple ways to start choosing from your heart rather than using your brain all of the time. When you say "I feel," you automatically move your decision making process from the brain to the heart. We are powerful beings and we can control our bodies with our words. When we use certain words like "I feel" we send a message to our body to use the heart for what comes next. After you say "I feel" just finish it with whatever comes up first. No need to analyze or ask why or to make sure. Our heart knows what it feels automatically and will not hesitate to let you know.

Our hearts truly do know what is best for us and will always lead us to where we need to be. It is true that our hearts can and will lead us to uncomfortable situations and pains, but that is because it knows that we are capable of overcoming these situations and growing to be stronger and better because of the experience. It will always give us the right answer and guide us in the right direction. The trick is that most of us do not trust our own hearts enough to follow it and we always doubt ourselves. We doubt our intuition and make choices based on fear instead of trusting that our hearts will lead us to where we need to be. It might be scary and unknown, but when you trust your heart to lead you, your life will begin to look different.

Our bodies are also great measuring sticks for how we feel. They are interconnected with the heart and can be trusted when they are sending us messages. For example, if when you make a decision you begin to get butterflies in your stomach or a headache, this could be a sign from your body saying that it is not the right decision. If you get goosebumps or the hair on your arms stands up it could be a sign that it is an exciting decision and you should move that way. Our bodies are talking to us and sending us messages all the time. They would never lie to us. It is important that we listen and trust our bodies.

Forgiveness is a key element to raising your emotional I.Q. All of us have faced a situation at some point in our lives in which forgiveness has played a role. Forgiveness is not just about releasing the other person from guilt but more importantly it is about allowing us to move on with our lives. Forgiveness helps to raise our vibration and allows for compassion and understanding to move in. In order to forgive we must be able to see the other side of the story and see our own role in the events. This will help us understand their actions from a different perspective.

I feel that I can safely say that not a single person has ever lived that has not had something happen to them where they have been faced with the choice of whether or not to forgive someone. When we choose not to forgive someone it does just as much damage to us as it does to them. We continue to carry negative energy towards them and we can stay stuck in the past. We will judge others based on what someone else did to us and this will have a negative effect on other relationships that had nothing to do with the initial hurt.

When we choose to move on and forgive someone it can be a great moment of release for both individuals. We no longer hold on to the energy or event of the past. We also release them of this negative energy too. We begin to heal the wound and start to reflect on what our role in the situation was. What was the lesson we needed to learn and how can we change to avoid the same type of situation in the future? Forgiveness is a healing process that allows us to move forward with light and energy instead of being held back by dark and fearful energy.

In order to forgive we must be able to view our situation from a couple different perspectives other than our usual one. First, it is important to understand what kind of state the other person was in when they made their decision. Maybe they were sad, or mad, or having a bad day. Maybe they do not view what they did as being wrong. Maybe they had something horrible happen to them and chose to pass that on to you. We never know unless we ask and make a choice to understand instead of getting mad and judging.

It is also just as important that we take a long hard look at how we played a role in the situation too. Many people might say that they played no role at all but this couldn't be further from the truth. If we played no role then we would not have been in the situation in the first place. Every choice we make, everything we do and say brings us to different experiences. Even the act of allowing a person into our lives that would do something to us is playing a role in the experience. By being at a certain place at a certain time is playing a role in an experience. If we have allowed people in the past to treat us in a certain way, maybe this person thought we were ok with being treated like that. When we are able to see that we played a role just as much as the one who sinned against us, then the healing process may begin.

Vulnerability is another key aspect of becoming comfortable with our emotions and raising our emotional I.Q. Vulnerability is when we allow ourselves to show emotion, express ourselves freely and openly with others and self without fear of what people may think or do to us. Most people choose how to show up to others very carefully as they do not want to offend anyone or want people to think badly of them. They don't want people to think they are weak or anything other than what they want to appear as.

When we allow ourselves to be vulnerable with others it shows great strength and courage. More importantly it shows that we are honest and authentic. People will definitely pick up on those traits and this will help build a strong foundation for any relationship. People can tell when someone is being fake or inauthentic and can really appreciate when someone is telling the truth. When you are vulnerable, you give off a certain type of energy that makes others feel warm, loving and compassionate.

When we are vulnerable, it allows for us to stop lying to ourselves and begin to be honest. For example, I used to always say that I didn't care about all the things my Dad did to me and my family and that I was fine without him. In short, he was abusive physically, mentally and emotionally. He left when I was still in elementary school. Once I was able to admit that I did care and that it did affect me, I was able to start moving to a place of healing instead of a place of avoidance. It allowed me to start being real with myself and stop putting on a mask to look strong in front of others. People either accepted it or not, that was not my concern. My concern was being able to show and say how I really felt in all situations no matter who I was dealing with. This way I would always be consistent and authentic and would start to be more comfortable with who I really am.

This allows others to also start to get to know who you really are. The consistency in your actions and words is key. Being vulnerable allows them to see that you are always the same. Most people show up with different personas or masks for different situations and for different people. People will pick up on the lack of consistency in your being and will not be as trusting of you. They will not connect as much with you and there will always be something in the way. When you begin to be the same no matter where or with who you are, trust will start to grow.

It is very important for us to be gentle when people come to us for forgiveness or when they are being vulnerable with us. Only the weak and scared choose to hurt others when they are at their most vulnerable. To kick someone when they are down takes no strength at all and is one of the most cowardly acts one can commit. The weak and scared choose to do this because they feel it will make them feel strong and powerful but they do not know it actually does the opposite. It just continues to feed the fear and anger. True strength comes from compassion, understanding and a willingness to be gentle. This is how we begin to heal the world and not just ourselves.

When dealing with others it is always easier to be gentle when you have the whole story. Many of us in western society decide that we do not need the whole story and like to fill in the holes and gaps with stories we make up in our own heads. It is always best to not assume anything and just ask the other person. This will avoid any unnecessary conflict and pain.

What I mean is that when we think people have wronged us we often do not have the whole story. For example, say someone said they were going to call us back but didn't, we start to feel wronged. Maybe they just forgot, maybe they had an emergency to deal with or there could be a million different reasons that have nothing to do with us that caused them to not call us back. Many people, myself included, would just make a story up like oh they didn't want to talk to me or I'm not important enough and start to feel angry or sad.

This is why whenever we start to have automatic reactions like this we should take a moment and step back. Do we know why they didn't call back? Are we making assumptions without having all the necessary information? When we do not have all the information it is always best to ask. For myself, in 95% of the situations where I have made assumptions about a particular event and then decided to ask, I was always wrong about their intentions. More often than not our assumptions are not based on fact. Asking will always clear things up and help keep peace in the relationship.

Honesty is something that everyone claims to want but few are willing to practice. True honesty is something we should strive to achieve. The more open and honest we can be with others and with ourselves, the higher the quality of our relationships will be. Honesty is a value that everyone holds in high esteem and is rarely looked down on. When people are asked what traits you would like your partner to have, honesty is always one of the top answers. No matter the kind of partner being talked about, honesty is an important trait when dealing with romance, business, sports or any other partnership.

Honesty is important to the success of any kind of relationship. I do not believe there exists a successful relationship anywhere that doesn't have honesty as a part of it. How could a relationship be successful without honesty? If you are being lied to and found out later on, would you consider that a successful relationship? Or the other way around if you are the one doing the lying, would you consider it successful? You might be temporarily getting what you want but it will not last forever and will come back around.

Honesty is the only foundation that a successful relationship can be built on. Anything else will wash away like sand when the tide sweeps in. Even in times where the truth can be painful it is best to still tell it. In the end, the other person will be grateful that you told the truth instead of a lie. The truth cannot be hidden for long and will only come out louder and stronger if an attempt is made to hide it.

There is another aspect that ties in with what I have been talking about. That is the giving yourself the permission and freedom to express yourself. We must be free to express ourselves in whatever way we see fit. This is very important. It is almost like we need to ask for permission from ourselves before we become so open, honest and vulnerable. I feel the reason it is this way is because we have buried and protected so many parts of ourselves for so long that it feels like it is against our own interests to be open with others. As if we are exposing ourselves to this great danger that lies in wait.

We will never be able to be honest and vulnerable without this freedom of expression. Honesty and vulnerability are exactly that, freedom of expression. Without this freedom we could never be able to tell the truth as it could hurt others or even hurt us. We could never be vulnerable as that could also hurt others and hurt us. When we give ourselves freedom we also give ourselves strength and confidence to endure and move on.

When we give ourselves freedom and live with this freedom we show others that it is possible to live open and free. By giving ourselves freedom we also give others this same freedom. If we create a safe space and environment for ourselves, others may also use this same safe place. Any freedoms we give to ourselves are in turn given to others. By lighting our own light we also light the world.

Taking negative emotions and turning them into something positive is one of the greatest strengths someone can have. This is called transmutation.

Transmutation has been around for thousands of years and is usually discussed when it comes to Alchemy. Alchemy is the art of taking base metals and turning them into gold. Transmutation with our emotions is the same concept except that we are not dealing with metals and instead dealing with emotions. There is no reason that we cannot take anger and turn it into a creative force or take sadness and turn it into motivation.

It helps us make the choice of how we want to feel in any given moment. If we do not like something then we can choose to not feel that way anymore and better yet put that energy into something that we do want to do. What better way to use our negative emotions than to use them as fuel to put into the things we do love?

For example, when I lose a soccer game and feel down, sad or angry I used to just go home to do nothing and be mad for literally days. I take my soccer very serious and let it get to me. Now I choose to act differently, as being angry for two or three days wasn't serving me particularly well. I now will go home and use that energy and start to work on one of my projects. Make a video, edit my website or something of the like. These have proven to be some of my most productive nights.

I am sure that most of you reading this book have heard of our "comfort zones." Our comfort zone is the space where we feel comfortable and not at risk to be judged or worried about anything. It is where we live most of our lives as our comfort zones keep us safe and away from anything that is a "risk" to us. Our comfort zones play a huge role in our emotional health as the more we stay in them the less we grow and evolve. The less we will be able to feel other feelings and have other experiences. The less we will see things from a different perspective and the less we will be able to understand about others. We will not be able to expand our context for life and will limit our lives to what we have already experienced.

When we are willing to take a risk and step outside of our comfort zone, that is when the magic starts to happen. We expand our context and open ourselves up to new experiences. We learn about new possibilities, we see from different perspectives and we get to experience life in a new way. Stepping out of the comfort zone is the best thing we can do to grow and evolve. It is like after a rubber band stretches, it never goes back to the same size it was before the stretching. This is the same for us. After we grow and evolve from our new experience we never go back to the old way of being and thinking.

This is why it is so important to continually push the limits and stretch your comfort zone as much as possible. We want to grow our context and experience as much as life has to offer. The more we grow and evolve the more we know and we find out that we have so much more growing to do. We see that there is so much more to life than what we thought and that life outside of our bubbles is so much more exciting. It is said that everything we want in life is waiting for us outside of our comfort zones.

I choose to consciously risk stepping out of my comfort zone on a regular basis. The feeling never changes for me either. I always feel nervous and I always feel scared too. Another thing that never changes is how I feel afterwards. After I am done, I always think to myself that it wasn't that bad. I find that the stories I tell myself in my head are never true and I always make it out to be worse than it actually is. I always feel so proud and energized after and this feeling tends to last for a while and spills into other areas of my life.

I also always learn something from taking these kinds of risks. I always learn that I am capable of much more than I give myself credit for. I learn that I have skills and traits that I never knew I had as I had never exercised those muscles before. I learn that when I put my mind to it I can accomplish anything I want. I learn about my willpower and determination and how much I truly want to change my life for the better. I learn something new every time.

There are many different ways to do this and it would be different for everyone. Something that would be out of my comfort zone could be like second nature to someone else. For example, I was usually pretty shy in my life and would rarely ever talk to people first, especially if it was a girl I was attracted to. So one day, I decided to go to the mall and find a woman I was especially attracted to and talk to her to get to know her without any motives. I was so scared and nervous, I walked by her twice before I actually sat down to talk to her. She was very receptive and we had a really good talk. I felt like a million dollars after and I feel like she gained from the experience as well. There are many guys reading this that may think that's not a big deal they do it all the time, but to me it was a big deal and I grew from that experience.

To be emotionally healthy we must allow ourselves the freedom to express. We must be open to being fully honest and vulnerable. We must be kind and willing to forgive. Most importantly, we must be willing to take risks and step out of our comfort zones. It is the only way we get to grow.

Chapter 6 - Trust

"I Trust You" is a better compliment than "I Love you" because you may not always trust the person you love but you can always love the person you trust
- Unknown

I feel that trust is such an important factor of our emotional I.Q that I am dedicating a whole chapter to it. What is trust though? Trust is a concept that entails a wide scale of meaning. To me trust is about letting people in even though there is the chance they can hurt you. Trust is allowing others to do what you need done without having to watch over them. Trust is about letting your guard down because you know you are in safe hands. Trust is about surrendering to life and going with the flow. Trust is believing in yourself, in others, in God and that you are where you are meant to be and you are being led to where you need to go. Trust is basically letting go and enjoying the ride.

Trust plays such an important part in our lives because it is one of the most sacred bonds in existence. Trust is what leads to love and without trust there can never be love. It plays a part in all kinds of relationships and when trust is broken it can destroy relationships, sometimes to the point where they cannot be repaired. Trust is crucial to friendships, family, business, and to all aspects of our lives.

Trust is one of the highest rated personal character traits one can possess and we all feel so much better when the one we are in a relationship with can be trusted. Trust makes us feel safe and secure. Trust allows us to be open, honest and vulnerable. It allows for relationships to go to the next level and have a deeper connection. There could never be a successful, happy, loving relationship without trust.

We all know what it is like to be able to trust someone and also what it is like for that trust to be violated. By knowing how it feels for trust to be broken it allows us to hold those that keep our trust that much closer and dearer to our hearts. It also allows us to strive to be trustworthy as we would never want someone to feel like we have broken their trust.

Trust is also one of the most delicate of all human values out there. Trust can be the easiest thing to lose and one of the hardest things to gain back.

There are many ways that trust can be lost. When someone shows up late, doesn't show up at all or forgets to get back to me when they said they would, I lose a little trust in them. If someone lies to me whether big or small I lose trust in them. If I feel like someone hasn't given 100% to a mutual project or wasn't authentic in our dealings I will lose trust in them. If I am working with someone and they stray from our game plan I will lose trust in them. Basically anytime that someone breaks an agreement we had I lose trust in them.

Once these people have crossed my line I feel that they must work 10x as hard to gain back my trust. I might be a bit of a hard ass but I feel safe when saying that for almost everyone it is true that if someone does something to break your trust it will be much harder to gain it back. I know there have been times where I broke trust with friends of mine. Times that I said I would go to a get together, or a birthday and even to help move and never showed up.

It is possible to gain trust back that has been lost. When someone tells us or we notice that we have broken their trust we can then consciously make a choice to do our best to repair that. Every person is different in how we are to gain their trust back. It is up to us to ask or find out what we can do to gain the trust back. We must be willing to put in the work before it is too late.

There are such accounts for keeping track of trust. These accounts are called Trust accounts. They work very similar to regular bank accounts in which there are deposits and withdrawals made regularly. Just like in a regular bank account it is important to keep a positive balance and not get overdrawn.

Trust accounts are usually not kept on paper or electronically like a bank account is. They are usually accounted for subconsciously and inside of us. We all have a line that cannot be crossed or a certain amount of trust that can be lost before we say no more. It also works the other way around. When we have an abundance of trust in our accounts, we may be more inclined to let things slide more than we usually would. Perhaps because these people have earned it or because we know that breaking trust is totally outside of their normal behavior.

It is important to be aware of these accounts and be aware that we do subconsciously keep track of where people are at. When we know this, we in turn also become aware that people have an account with our name on it as well. Every time we earn or lose trust with others it is being tracked by those individuals as well. This will allow us to become more conscious of the effect our choices have on others and the consequences of the choices we make.

There are large and small transactions that have different effects on the balance of the account. For example, being late to a dinner could be a small withdrawal while not showing up at all could be a large withdrawal from the account. A small deposit could be that you were there to take a call when someone needed a person to listen to them. A large deposit could be that you drove out to the middle of nowhere in the middle of the night to help fix a flat tire. This will vary from person to person but the concept will be the same. Some actions will be withdrawals and some actions will be deposits.

Most of us, in some way, know what the trust balance is for each person we are in a relationship with. It is important to have this kind of awareness when it comes to our relationships. When people's trust accounts are close to being overdrawn we could have a conversation with them to let them know how their actions are affecting us. Conversely, when people have an abundance of trust in their accounts with us we could take them for dinner or a show to express our gratitude for them being so awesome. Trust works both ways and it is important to let people know how they are doing with us.

There are some key ways to make sure you are making more deposits than withdrawals. These ideas can help make sure your relationships are of a higher quality. The first idea is keeping the agreements you make with others and with yourself. The second idea is the art of renegotiation. They are both really important and can play a huge role in making sure you always have an abundance of trust in all of your accounts.

Agreements are pretty much equivalent to financial transactions. An agreement that is followed is considered to be a deposit and an agreement that is broken is considered to be a withdrawal. The reason is because agreements are when we give our word to another that we are going to do something for them. Our word is the foundation of what trust is built upon. People trust us when we keep our word and people lose trust when we break our word. We also make agreements with ourselves all the time that we must be aware of too. An example is something as simple as I am going to wake up at 8 a.m. tomorrow morning. If we do not get up until 9 a.m. that is considered a broken agreement with self.

At this point, you might be thinking that there is no way you could possibly keep all the agreements you make. Life happens and sometimes things don't go as planned. I totally agree and that is why it is important to become aware of the art of renegotiation. For example, let's say that you are to meet a friend at 2 p.m. for lunch. You are on your way but then you get a flat tire and know you are not going to be able to make it on time. What do you do? Do you just deal with the flat tire and call them afterwards to explain? In my eyes, that would constitute a broken agreement as they could be at the restaurant waiting for you. Another action is that you could call them and let them know about your situation. Ask them if it is ok if you are late or if you guys pick another occasion to meet. Get agreement from them about what the new agreement will be and this way both parties can be satisfied with the way it turns out and no one is left with any trust withdrawals.

Renegotiation really is this simple and can be done in a matter of a few minutes. You are not breaking an agreement because you have let them know that something came up and replaced the old agreement with a new one. It is much better than breaking an agreement and trying to fix it afterwards. If we could all be aware of this concept and how powerful it truly is we would be involved in healthier relationships with others and with ourselves.

This is how keeping agreements and using the art of renegotiation can be important concepts to lead us towards healthier relationships. It is important not to abuse renegotiation or people will not trust your process. Being open, honest, and authentic is the only way to be when using renegotiation. We should always strive to do our best and make agreements we are sure we can keep in the first place.

I feel like most people would agree when I say that actions are more important than words. Words are just words. It is nice to hear the things we want to hear, it helps us feel happy and secure. When those words are found to be lies though, the results can be devastating. Many people use words to manipulate others and to take advantage of others. I know because I have done it. I have told women many lies about how I felt about them in order to get something out of them. When they would find out it was just words, the consequences were never pretty. This is just one example of many that could fit this idea. It happens in all kinds of relationships and not just our primary relationships.

If you tell someone you miss them but do not make the effort to see them, your actions are really saying I do not miss you. If you tell someone you miss them and then go out of your way, even if it means losing sleep, money or time to see them then your actions are in alignment with your words. When your actions and words are in alignment, it has a profound impact on the person to which you are giving. It shows them that you are genuine, authentic and trustworthy. Alignment of our actions with our words is what we should strive to achieve.

In the end when looking back it is very difficult to remember what people say to us. In the same sense it is difficult to even remember what we say to other people too. It is much easier to remember what people did and how they made us feel. How many times have you recalled an event and talked about how you felt and what the other people involved were doing? This happens with much more frequency than being able to recall what people say to us. The actions form a deeper relationship to how we feel and also to our memories. Emotions are tied to our memories better than words are and this is why it is easier to remember how people made us feel than to try and recall what they said to us.

Communication is another key aspect of being able to build trust in relationships. I feel that open and honest communication is an excellent way to build trust. When we trust the person we are in a relationship with we should feel safe to say what we need to say. Communicating how we feel, what we need and what we expect is crucial to being successful. We should not expect anyone to just figure it out on their own. When people do not get the required information they just make assumptions which are, more often than not, incorrect. It is important that we leave nothing to chance or to assumptions and to communicate in a clear and concise manner.

On the other side of giving an open and honest message we must be willing and able to listen. Most people in our society listen to respond. That is, they are just waiting for the other person to stop talking so they can give their response. It is important that we make the move and begin listening to understand. Truly hearing the other person's words and understanding what they are saying. This requires us to not form judgements or analyze what they are saying while they are saying it. Being present to them and showing them that we are indeed hearing what they are saying.

A key part to add on to that is about clarifying questions. If we do not understand what someone has said we should not leave the conversation without clarifying. It is not wise to walk away and make assumptions about what they might have said. We could say to them, what I think I heard you say is... and check in with them if that is the correct message they were trying to convey. You could even just simply ask what did you mean by that or I do not understand, can you say it in a different way? There are many ways to let them know you do not understand and that you would like them to clarify so that you truly know what they meant. This is the best way to make sure you understand the other person and what they are trying to say to you.

When you are building trust with people you want to make sure you are setting yourself up for success. What I mean is, for example, if you are in money trouble and need to borrow $500, ask someone that you know has extra money saved and not someone that is also in money trouble. Asking someone who cannot deliver will get you a no response and you will feel let down that they did not come to your aid. This is a factor that many people do not think about. We usually just ask the people that we feel should help us without thinking about whether they have the capacity to actually help.

You must also be the kind of person that has built enough trust that they feel ok with lending you the money. If you have a habit of not paying people back then they are less likely to come to your financial aid. It is important to set ourselves up for success by asking the right people and by being trustworthy ourselves. This will go a long way in making sure that we have successful relationships with others.

First of all, you need to be clean and clear about what it is exactly that you are in need of. If you do not know what you want then how can you expect someone else to deliver? It is really important to take the time to check in with yourself and really understand what it is you are going to be asking for. When you find out what you need then it is important to be able to clearly communicate this to the person you are asking so that they understand your need. It is just as important for you to understand your own need as it is for the other person to understand your need as well.

Next you must know what the people you are asking for help are capable of delivering. If you have two different friends in which one is a good listener and empathetic and the other is loud and energetic, you are going to ask them for different kinds of support. The good listener can come in handy when you are feeling down and need to vent to someone. The loud and energetic friend could be excellent if you have an important soccer game and would like some loud and excited fans there to cheer you on. Both friends would then feel proud that they were able to come to your aid when you needed it. It would be unwise to ask your loud and energetic friend to come over and hang out when you are in need of a quiet night in. We want to set our friends up for success just as much as we should set ourselves up for success too.

Everyone needs different kinds of support and everyone has different ways of giving support. Some people need money, some people need someone to vent to and some just need a cheerleader in their corner. Some ways that I offer support to my friends is by being a good listener and helping them come up with solutions to their problems. I have been told my presence can be very calming and helps people relax and not be so worried. Find what kind of support works for you and then ask for it. If you do not ask then you will not get it.

Next I want to talk about a few different kinds of trust and how they differ from each other. Trust looks different in each kind of relationship depending on who it is with.

Self-trust is perhaps one of the most important ways that trust can show up. I really feel that if we are to trust others and have them trust us we must first start with trusting ourselves. It sounds so simple but many people actually do not trust themselves. Have you ever gotten excited about a new idea only to let your mind talk you out of it? Have you ever wanted to go tryout for a team and not go because you thought you weren't good enough? All of these are examples of possible signs of not trusting yourself. Once we truly trust ourselves we will always be willing to risk comfort in order to go for what we really want. Whether we get it or not doesn't matter as we will grow and evolve as a result of the decision to go for it. When we trust ourselves we feel the fear and do it anyways. When we trust ourselves it is obvious to other people and therefore it becomes easier for them to trust us as well.

Whether we trust ourselves or not will be evident in other areas of our lives too. If we do not trust ourselves it will show up loudly in our relationships. We will be hesitant to show up authentically and genuine and will want to keep people at a distance. We will put on masks and act differently all the time depending on who we are with. We will even do things we wouldn't normally do and that might go against our morals just to be accepted and fit in. Our words and actions may not be in alignment and we might be pretending so much that we forget who we truly are. There are a lot of ways that a lack of self-trust can show up. I know this because for most of my life I didn't trust myself.

When we do trust ourselves there can be some really cool benefits as well. We will start to experience deeper connections with the people we are in relationships with. A deeper level of understanding and intimacy that isn't available until there is a deep level of trust. We will have new experiences when we are able to let go and be fully vulnerable with another person and just go with the flow of that experience. When we allow people to see us for who we truly are they will allow us to see them for who they truly are which creates a deeper connection.

One of the biggest aspects of self-trust is trusting your intuition. Trusting your intuition is one of the bravest and most rewarding things you can do. It can also be one of the hardest levels of trust to get to. Once you are at a place where you fully trust your intuition your life will start to move with you instead of against you.

Trusting your intuition does take a lot of courage and bravery to do especially when starting out. Most of us have been taught to follow orders and do as we are taught in school and some people aren't even aware that we have intuition. To me our intuition is our soul speaking to us and guiding us. It gives us subtle hints and clues that, if we pay attention to, can lead us to wonderful experiences. It can be difficult to trust our intuition because it is the unknown and often leads us to things we have never done before. We just need to trust that our soul would never lead us in the wrong direction.

When we fight or resist our intuition, life becomes hard as we are going against the flow that our soul has intended for us. It can be frustrating and we can be left wondering as to why life has been so bad to us. The benefits of this trust is that when we make a decision to follow our intuition it almost seems as if even mountains are willing to move out of the way in order for us to get what we want. Sometimes, we don't know how but things come to us with more ease and abundance. We stop worrying about the process and enjoy the ride that we call life.

If you are in a primary relationship that lacks trust then that can be a recipe for disaster. There will be constant fights and worrying about what they are doing when you are not together. Are they cheating or doing other things behind your back? Do they have a separate life that you do not know about? The list is endless of things that can go wrong and it isn't all about cheating. It can also be about not allowing them close to you and making them feel unwanted and unworthy. Making your partner feel unloved can have a big impact on them and you. There is not much good that can come from being in a primary relationship that isn't built on trust.

On the other hand there can be a level of intimacy that could never be matched in any other relationship if you trust the person you are with. Your souls can connect in a way in which you feel like one. You get to reach a level that is much more than just physical. You begin to touch each other mentally, emotionally and spiritually. The relationship can become fun and help both of you grow and evolve at a rate that is beyond what is possible on your own.

Trust with family and friends will determine the quality of those relationships. We do not pick our family but we do pick our friends. When we are able to trust the people that make up our lives, we can live much happier lives and have the support we need to grow and prosper.

Trusting our family is almost a given. They are the ones that have been there from the start and for the most part will always be there. A strong family bond is built on trust. They know you for who you are and know you at your best and worst. This is one of the most delicate forms of trust there is. They know your strengths and weaknesses and what buttons to push. I feel that we learn at a pretty young age whether to trust our families with that kind of power or not. When we are able to trust our family members it is a bond that will last a lifetime.

Our friends are like the family that we get to choose. Our friends get the privilege of knowing us in ways that sometimes even our own families do not know. We show them a side of us that is reserved for the special ones in whom we place that level of trust. Different friends will see us in a different light depending on the type of relationship. Again, we learn pretty quickly who can and cannot be trusted with our intimate knowledge. Friendships will be tested and those who pass the test can also form relationships that last a lifetime. We do not need to talk to or see our friends all the time but once that bond is formed it never goes away.

When we have family and friends in our lives that we can fully trust life becomes a lot easier and happier. We have people to lean on whenever times get tough and people that can support us in any way we need. We are also able to offer support to them when they need it. There has to be a balance in the giving and taking of support in order for the relationship to work. When we have this balance it allows the relationship to grow and prosper. I believe that to be truly happen we need to have these kinds of people in our lives.

There are also times where we will need to work in a group environment such as sports, work or school. It is important that there is a mutual trust of each other and if there is a leader that this person is also trusted. Depending on the situation in which we are working there can be big risks involved. There can be dangerous work environments or even in sports people can get injured when their teammate makes a mistake. A great deal of trust needs to be in place in order to keep a group environment safe and successful. If trust doesn't exist with even just one of the group members it can lead to risky business.

Even in our social circle there will be times where we need to work with others that we may or may not know. An example could be a fundraiser project, a surprise party for a friend or planning a special event. This kind of trust usually has minimal levels of risk but it is still there. People's feelings can get hurt and trust can be broken. Sometimes it is even more rewarding when you accomplish goals with people you do not really know well as it helps build your trust, faith, and confidence in people and humanity in general. It can be a beautiful thing when people come together for a common goal and everyone leaves having had fun and grown from the experience.

Surrender is something that can help us achieve the levels of trust that we aspire to reach. Surrender is the act of stopping the resistance we put up against what happens in life. What we resist persists. When we surrender we are telling life that we accept what has happened, accept that we cannot change what happened and that we are ready to move forward. We do not always know what moving forward means but we know that it means we are leaving behind the situation we are currently in.

This is where the trust part comes in. Surrender and trust go hand in hand. When we surrender to moving forward we must trust that we are being led to where we need to be and when we need to be there. There is no guarantee that it will be easy and more often than not it isn't easy but it will be rewarding and fulfilling. The person you will become will thank you for taking the risk and allowing yourself to grow and evolve.

Trust and surrender are usually more about the long term than the short term gain. The rewards will not come overnight and we must remain consistent and determined to see our process through. It is almost like a test that we must go through in order to reach our fullest potential. If it was easy then it wouldn't be as rewarding when we arrive at our destination. Stay in it for the long run and you will not be disappointed.

I feel like faith is the ultimate level of trust. There is nothing higher than faith when it comes to trust. Faith is so important because it is trusting in that which can never be known. That which cannot be seen and cannot be proven, yet it can be felt deep in our hearts. We all feel it from time to time. This energy, this force. It is the goosebumps we get or when our hairs on our arms all stand up when something amazing has just happened. That feeling we get when we meet someone for the first time that we feel like we have known for a lifetime. That feeling we get when life takes a turn for the best and everything starts to conspire for us.

Faith is about moving forward with trust and without knowing what is ahead. It is about trusting that this higher power would not walk us off a mountain but instead would build a magnificent staircase for us to climb higher than we have ever imagined. Again, trusting that this force is here to support us and would never lead us astray.

So what is this power and force that I keep referring to? It is God, of course. This force has been given many names over the millennia and for the purpose of ease I will refer to it as God. It has also been called the universe, love, consciousness, energy, spirit and a whole other myriad of names. For now, I would just like to acknowledge that there is a force out there bigger than any one of us that is here to support us if we allow it to.

Part 4
Spiritual Abundance

Chapter 7 – Spirituality

Zen does not confuse spirituality with thinking about God while one is peeling the potatoes. Zen spirituality is just to peel the potatoes
- Alan Watts

To me, spirituality is an awareness of the bigger picture and what role we have to play in that bigger picture. It is an awareness that there is a force or energy out there that is bigger than all of us and that it is here to support us. Spirituality is an awareness of who we truly are and the infinite potential that lies within all of us. It is about realizing our true power and using it to better our lives and the lives of everyone around us. Spirituality is realizing that we are here for a reason and that there are no accidents or coincidences. It is about knowing that we are all individuals, yet, at the same time we are all connected as one.

Spirituality is the essence of life and to be successful in life we must be aware that we all have a spiritual side. Whether we acknowledge this side of ourselves or not it will have a guiding hand in every aspect of our lives. Spirituality will be there to give us gut feelings about new people we meet or situations we find ourselves in. It will be there to guide us to experiences we were meant to have so that we can grow and evolve in the way we need to.

When we acknowledge this we allow this energy to move through us and support us in any way that we see fit. We become one with the world and begin to live in harmony with our environment. I am not saying that life becomes perfect and we will never have another problem again. What I am saying is that we will have a better understanding of life and why things happen the way that they do. We will have the support we need to move through life with purpose and passion and the energy needed to accomplish our goals. We will have a clearer perspective of the world and be able to relate to other people in a new and more profound way.

I would like to start with saying that there are some key differences between religion and spirituality. Spirituality is more about freedom and finding your own way to the truth. I am a firm believer that all paths eventually lead to the same place. Some paths will take longer and have more twists and turns but eventually we will all end up in the same place. It can be no other way. So yes, religion and spirituality will lead you to the same place but they will be two entirely different journeys full of different kinds of experiences.

With saying that, I feel the need to say that you do not have to be religious to be spiritual. This does not mean that you cannot be both religious and spiritual at the same time. You can be both and you can be either or and you also be neither. That is the wonderful part of the human experience. We have free will to choose to be anything we want to be. Some people start out as religious and then become spiritual. Some people go the other way and start off as spiritual and then become religious. So it is very possible for a person to be spiritual without being religious. There are no rules to this and no right and wrong way to be. It is your journey and only you know what is best for you. I like a quote by Alan Watts that I feel sums it up perfectly. "Someone that tells you that he has some way of leading you to spiritual enlightenment is like someone who picks your pocket and sells you your own watch."

For myself, I was half religious as a kid. I went to church sometimes and went to a Catholic school but didn't necessarily buy into the whole program. I then turned away from religion completely and just drifted for a while before finding my way to spirituality. I took a dangerous route as I chose to live a high risk lifestyle and never thought about the future. I lived day by day and had zero purpose and awareness of the bigger picture. I do not regret anything as it allowed me to have a different experience of life than most people.

It did allow me to live outside of the norms of our society and do things my own way. In doing this, I had a lot of freedom. This caused me to seek out answers to the big questions in life outside of the normal realms that most people would seek them out. I did my own research and digested as much information as I could. I read as many philosophical, historical and "controversial" books as I could get my hands on. I watched documentaries and pretty much listened to everyone I could listen to including the Jehovah's Witness that would knock on my door every weekend. I then made up my own mind and kept walking my own path. I feel like that is my path to truth. Listen to everyone and then make up my own mind about what I choose to believe and take in.

Today I would definitely consider myself to be spiritual and to have my own way of practicing so that I keep my connection strong and lasting. I have never been a believer in that there is only one way of doing things and I like to live life on my own terms. I believe this way of living is what lead me down the path to spirituality. This is the way I will continue to live and if I have children it will be the way I wish they live but will not force anything upon them. If I am to be remembered for anything I wish it to be as someone that lived life on his own terms and by doing so gave others the freedom to do so as well.

So what is this big picture that I keep referring to? What exactly do I mean and what does it have to do with living a balanced life? What role is it that we as individuals have to play in this bigger picture?

I feel like the big picture is pretty easy to explain conceptually but can be challenging to grasp. The big picture is simply just an awareness that there is more to this world than you and I. There is more to the world than what we are able to perceive through our five senses. There is something else that binds us all together and keeps everything in a perfect balance. It was no accident that the right conditions came about on this planet for life to thrive in the manner that it has. The odds are beyond astronomical that something like this could have taken place by a mere accident.

I feel like this is a big part of living a balanced life. When we become aware that there is more to our lives than just what we experience on a day to day basis it gives us purpose and meaning. I find great comfort in the fact that this was all created for us to have the experiences we are having and that I am a part of something much greater than I can even begin to imagine. The bigger picture helps keep me grounded and it helps me feel safe at times when things are not going as well. When I look out at nature or at the stars and know that they are just as much a part of me as my arms and legs, I get a feeling of peace and that everything is going to be just fine. In fact, it is going to be even better than I can imagine. This helps me stay on track in life and helps me to keep moving forward.

As individual people, what role can we possibly play in this bigger picture? My answer is that we are all helping to create this universe and molding it into the kind of place that we want it to be. Every act, thought and emotion sends out a ripple effect into the world that is felt by everyone and thing. Also, when we feel that we are a part of the bigger picture, we start to feel a greater appreciation and sense that we need to take care of our environment. It changes our outlook on life and the way we behave. We no longer want to pollute the world as we understand we are only polluting ourselves. When we feel connected to everything we start to treat everyone and thing as if they were one of our own. As if they were part of our family or even as how we want to be treated.

There is a very important concept that I would like to introduce now as I feel that it goes a long way in helping us connect to our spirituality and the bigger picture. This is the concept of being the observer to our thoughts, emotions and actions. To be the observer sounds pretty simple but it is not that easy. When you are having thoughts, any kind of thoughts, just take a step back and observe without judgement or attaching any value to the thoughts. Just simply notice what you are thinking. The same with when you react to events or people. Simply just notice how you are reacting without judging it to be good or bad. This can be done with any situation, thought or emotion. The most important part of being the observer is to just notice what you are doing and to place no judgement on any of it. Simply observe.

When we are able to simply observe and not judge, it allows us to become more aware of who we are and of what is driving us. The things we notice about ourselves can be huge clues as to what belief systems we have working in the background of our minds. These beliefs are what are subconsciously running the show. When we can begin to identify them we can begin to choose whether they are serving us or not. If they are not we can make the conscious choice to change them. We will notice what our automatic reactions to certain situations are and we will begin to notice patterns in our thoughts, actions and words.

Once we have made the observations and discoveries about our belief systems we get to the fun part. When we decide if they are serving us or whether we want new beliefs to replace the ones that are not serving us. When we replace old beliefs with new ones we are able to experience life from a different perspective and have different experiences. We live from a different energy and see things like they are brand new to us. This can be a very exciting time as it is like a veil that was blinding us for so long has finally been lifted and we can now see clearly.

We are all here for a reason. It is not an accident that you are here on Earth at this time or even reading these words at this moment. It is all done on purpose and by design. We all have different reasons for coming here but we also share the same end goal. I believe that end goal is to grow and evolve to a point where we will feel that we do not need to come back anymore. This could take a long time to do but in the grand scheme of things it is not that long at all.

Throughout life we will have many different people cross our paths and will have many different experiences. We should take notice when certain experiences or people get us excited and seem to light a fire inside of us. These can be clues as to what our purpose in this lifetime could be. For myself, I get really excited when I get to talk to people about a book I just read or about a documentary I just watched. I love having deep, meaningful conversations with people and uncovering things I never knew before. This has led me to discover that my reason for being here is to walk my own path and teach people how to do the same. I am a forever student and teacher. Always seeking out new experiences and then sharing them with anyone who is willing to listen. I am here to show people that there is a different way of thinking, acting and most importantly, a different way of being.

I have known about my purpose for a few years now and have not really embraced it until recently. I have been scared of my purpose for just as long as I have known about it. The usual doubts like why would people listen to me or who am I to show people a different way have been my biggest obstacles to overcome. It takes a lot of courage to step into your purpose and live it. For many of us, myself included, we have been living our lives in the opposite manner of what our true purpose is. Our purpose can feel foreign and we do not have the slightest idea on how to achieve it or how to even begin to embody it. I feel like the first step is to acknowledge your purpose and say yes to it. Then surrender to your purpose and trust that it will lead you to where you need to be.

Once we are able to find our purpose and acknowledge it, we can begin to live a life that is more in alignment with that purpose. We will start to make changes that will help us move forward with our lives. We will feel energized and have a new zest for life. Our purpose will be what helps us stay up late and get up early. It will be what drives us forward.

When I found my purpose I began to take a look around my life and noticed that I was not living a lifestyle that was in alignment with my purpose. My purpose is to be a teacher and show people a new way of being. Yet, when I discovered this I was still spending lots of time at the bar getting drunk and smoking cannabis every single day. I was spending time with people who were not good influences and who lowered my vibration. I wasn't meditating, I wasn't volunteering and I definitely wasn't living my purpose.

I first began to be more selective with who I was spending time with. I heard a phrase that really had a big impact on my life. You are the average of the five people you spend the most time with. This phrase changed my life. I looked at who I was spending time with and was not surprised to see where I was at in life. Next, I decided to start on my goal of teaching others and started a blog. Then down the road that led to me starting a YouTube channel. I started taking personal development classes and spending time with people that wanted more out of life too. People that were striving to become more and be better than they were yesterday. As I am writing these words, I have not smoked cannabis in over three months and have only drank once in the last eight months. I have made many changes in my life to allow me to experience life in a way that would help me embody my purpose of living.

When I began to make these changes I felt like a new person was born. I had a new energy that I had not had before. This is what keeps me going when I begin to doubt myself or when I feel like quitting. It is what helps me say no to jobs and other opportunities that would only be short term solutions and would cause me to stray from my purpose. My purpose gave me the confidence to keep walking into the unknown and to not be afraid of what might happen. I knew that if I just kept going that things would turn out ok. I never felt like this before.

Now I work on my purpose every single day. Even the days that I do not want to work on it and would rather just sit around and do nothing. The days that I don't feel good or am tired I still do something to get me closer to my dreams. As I do something every day it adds to my energy and to my enthusiasm and lust to go for my dreams. It builds momentum that allows me to function on less sleep and still have the energy to do it. It helps me get out of my comfort zone by helping me focus on how much closer I will be rather than focusing on the fear side of it.

This purpose has lit a fire inside of me that can never be put out.

I believe that we are all creators and that life isn't happening to us it is happening through us. We are each creating our own realities through our beliefs and choices we make. By choosing to change our beliefs we also choose to create a new reality instead of staying with the one we continue to create.

The fact that we are creating our experiences might be hard for people to grasp as they might ask why we would ever choose to have bad things happen to us. I will share an example from my own life that will help make my point clearer. When I was young I formed a belief that stayed with me until recently. This belief was that relationships do not work. Therefore, throughout my life I was guided towards situations and experiences that would reinforce this belief. I was rarely ever in a primary relationship and saw many relationships fail and fail disastrously too. I had friends betray my trust. I saw people cheat on each other. I saw abusive relationships and I saw people constantly fighting.

Everywhere I looked I saw failed relationships and I always thought "that's why I am single." We must remember that our belief system serves two purposes. The first is to keep us safe and the second is to make us right. By guiding me to see failed relationships wherever I looked and causing me to stay away from relationships, my belief system did its job perfectly. I was never cheated on, I was never abused and so on. I was safe from the doom and gloom of a relationship and I was right about relationships not working.

This is just a brief explanation and example of how we are creators that create our own realities. Now imagine had I had a different belief system that said relationships do work and can be very rewarding. Do you think my life would have been different than it was? The beauty of this is that we all have a choice on whether we want to continue with the beliefs we have or if we want to create a new reality for ourselves. I have chosen to create a new reality by becoming aware of limiting beliefs like "relationships don't work" and consciously choosing to change them. This can have a profound impact on your life as it has on my own.

Our thoughts are another way in which we create our reality. Many people do not realize how powerful our thoughts really are. There is a lot of energy behind our thoughts and that energy is used to attract what we are thinking about. I am sure that we have all had that experience where we were thinking about someone and all of a sudden we get a text or phone call from them. This is a simple example of how our thoughts are used to create our realities.

I would also like to clarify that our brains do not distinguish between I want item A and I do not want item A. All our brains see is item A and that is what it is going to bring into our realities. I bring up this point so that we can learn how to better direct our energy. For example, if we want there to be peace in the world, we should not be anti-war. Instead we should be pro-peace. By being anti-war we are still thinking of war and giving our energy to those kinds of thoughts. By making the simple, yet powerful change, of being pro-peace we are now giving our energy and thoughts to what we really want. This simple technique can help you get more of what you truly want in life.

If you really want help in manifesting your desires you should start to attach emotion to your thoughts. For example, if you want to win your soccer game and you are thinking about winning it, start to think about how it will feel to win the game. Start to think about how awesome it will feel to score the winning goal and how your team will feel after the win. Our brains give out very powerful magnetic fields that attract these things to us but our heart's magnetic field is infinitely more powerful. This is why when we attach emotion to our thoughts we have a much better chance of getting what we want. Let your heart and brain work together to bring you what you want.

Often times, when I have conversations with people, about spirituality, they want to talk about what is right and wrong for spiritual people to do. I am here to set the record straight and say that there is no such thing as right and wrong. It is all based on our perspectives and judgements. We can only continue to evolve and grow and accordingly change our behaviors to fit our new level of understanding.

Did I really just say that there is no such thing as right and wrong? Let me explain myself first. I believe that we are all doing the best we can with where we are at in our personal evolution. There are some things I did in my past that, with what I now know, I would definitely judge as being bad. However, at the time I did these things I did not know what I know now and was acting from a lower level of consciousness. At the time, I felt like what I was doing was ok and was totally justified because of the experiences I had in life up until that point. To put it simply, I didn't know any better. Once I did know better I chose to not behave in that way anymore.

Right and wrong is all based on perspective. What you deem to be right could be totally wrong to me based on my perspective. What I say is right could be totally wrong from your perspective. How do we draw a line when we all have different perspectives, beliefs, and experiences? We are all at different stages of evolution and could not possibly expect to be on the same level of understanding with what other people think is right and wrong.

We must continue on our own path of growth and evolution and continue to learn new ways on being and understanding. As we grow and evolve, our behaviors will also change. This does not mean that the old behaviors were right or wrong but that we now have a better understanding of life and choose to act in a new way. As our understanding grows we will also judge other people's actions less and less. Who are we to judge what anyone else has done when we do not know their story or where they are in their own evolution. All we can do is to shine our light and set a good example.

To continue down this path of setting the record straight I would also like to say that there is no Heaven and Hell. Just like right and wrong, this is all based on our perspective. There is no judgement day awaiting those that have sinned and no eternal damnation for those judged to be bad. There is also no Heaven awaiting those that have not sinned or have had their sins forgiven. Heaven and Hell are what we make them to be and both can be experienced right here on Earth.

Hell is what we experience here on Earth when we decide to cut ourselves off from the divine and turn a blind eye to who we truly are. Hell is when we go through life thinking things just happen to us and not realizing that we are the ones creating our reality. Hell is when we choose to go through life alone instead of connecting with everything around us. Hell is living life just to go to work and pay bills. Hell is not knowing our purpose in life and just wandering around resisting whatever comes our way. Always asking "why me?" and playing the victim. Hell is what we make it out to be.

Heaven can truly be lived here on Earth during this current lifetime. Heaven is when we realize we have the power to create any reality we choose to and use that power to live out our dreams. Heaven is when we build a community of loving and supportive individuals who accept us for who we are. Heaven is accepting others for who they are and supporting them too. Heaven is loving the life you live and giving back to your community and the world whenever you can. Heaven is when you feel the connection to the divine and you live your purpose. Heaven can and is lived here on Earth. It is simply a choice that needs to be made.

Both Heaven and Hell can be experienced here on Earth in this lifetime by the same individual. In fact many people do experience both. Sometimes it takes going through Hell to be able to experience Heaven. God gave us free will for a reason and it would be ludicrous to think that this same God that gave us free will would then punish or reward us for using that free will. Heaven and Hell are based on our individual perspective just like right and wrong. A child in a war-torn country could think our lives are heavenly while a child here, in Canada, could think it is hell because he didn't get the new X-box for Christmas. It is all merely perspective.

With saying that there is no Heaven and Hell I am not by any means trying to say that there is no God or that we do not have a soul or anything of that matter. I strongly feel that we all do, in fact, have a soul. I feel that our soul is constantly communicating with us and giving us inspiration. Our souls are here to evolve as souls just as much as we evolve as humans throughout our physical life.

I feel that the question of whether we all have souls or not shouldn't even be a question. We all definitely do have souls. That might be hard to scientifically prove but once you have had the privilege of getting to know your soul you know that it is absolutely true. There are many ways to experience your soul. Meditation, near-death experiences, praying, and so many other ways that could fill a book themselves. Out of body experiences are probably one of the more common ways that people experience this. I feel like that is enough evidence for the soul as how else could we leave the body if we did not have a soul?

Our souls are what connect us to the divine. Whenever we get a gut feeling or goosebumps or other signs, that is our soul sending us a message. When we get ideas and inspiration, that is our soul talking to us. The very word inspiration means in spirit. That is not a coincidence. Our soul is sending us signs all the time, we just need to take the time to slow down and listen. It will guide us in the right direction.

Once we can accept the fact that we all have souls we can move on to the next part of our evolution. This is the concept of oneness. That we are all one. We are all connected and part of something much bigger than any individual. What we do to others, we are also doing to ourselves. When we truly understand this concept, our perceptions and behaviors will begin to shift.

Our souls are what connect us to each other and are the smaller parts of the whole. It is similar to how each of us has billions of cells that make up our body. Billions of souls and other energies make up God, Consciousness or whatever name you want to give it. It is the only way that God could experience all parts of itself. It is one thing to know that you are everything but it is a total other thing to experience everything. This is why God would want to do this in the first place. This concept is so grand in its design that it can be hard to understand and to take in. It is true though and it is possible to have experiences that connect you to this truth.

I feel that this is where the Golden Rule comes from. Do unto others as you would want done unto you. In other words, how we treat others is how we will be treated. This is exactly what it means to be one. What you put out will come right back to you as it cannot go anywhere else. There is nowhere else for it to go. This is how empaths are able to feel what other people feel.

When we begin to understand this our lives will definitely change. When we understand that we are one and that everything on the outside is as much a part of us as our arms and legs then we will never want to hurt anyone again. We will make conscious choices and think about the consequences of our actions before we act. We will be careful about the kind of energy we put out into the world and will want to always act from a place of love rather than a place of fear. We will treat everyone as if they were us or our family because in the end they truly are.

There is an energy that keeps us all connected and can be accessed by us. Meditation is the best way that I am aware of to tap into this energy. When we silence our minds and bodies we make room for other things to come in. We feel the energy that surrounds us and allow it to fill us with confidence and love. We allow it to energize and inspire us. This is another reason as to why meditation is so important for us to take part in.

Before I end this chapter on spirituality I would like to briefly mention the spirit world. Although we cannot see, hear or feel the Spirit World, I can assure you it does exist. There are many stories of people who died and have come back with amazing stories of what they experienced on the other side. There are people who do past life regressions who can confirm the existence of this other world. There are even hypnotherapists now who do "life between lives" hypnotherapy that have taken our understanding of the spirit world to a whole new level. Dr. Newton is one such hypnotherapist that has done amazing work in this field.

In the spirit world we will find a whole myriad of characters that reside there. The most commonly known ones would be the angels. Ranging from arch angels to our guardian angels and others. There will be our spirit guides which can best be described as the ones who help our soul on its journey of evolution. Similar to a mentor in the physical world that would help us evolve through life. There are soul families which are groups of souls in which we incarnate with over several lifetimes. Also, our own soul resides here too. Since we are infinite in nature, it is possible for our soul to reside with us in the physical and also in the spirit world at the same time.

The spirit world is pretty much where home is for all of us. This is where we go when we die and where we spend our time before deciding to come back to Earth for some more lessons. It very much is a choice to come back, just as everything else is also a choice. The spirit world is where we go to recharge and to regain clarity. To remember everything that we forgot the last time we came to the Earth. It is where we reflect on how we did in our physical incarnation and where we prepare for our next one.

Chapter 8 – The Signs

Coincidence is God's way of remaining anonymous
- Albert Einstein

The spirit world is communicating with us all the time. It communicates to us through signs it sends. The signs are being sent to support us. We need to be able to recognize them as signs from the divine and be willing to receive them. These signs can help point us in the right direction if we are brave enough to follow them.

The spirit world wants to help us succeed in life and reach our fullest potential for our current lives. The only problem is that they are not supposed to directly intervene in our lives. There are exceptions to this rule but generally speaking they stick to their world and we stick to ours. This is why they send us signs instead of just coming here and telling us directly. It is their way of reaching out and supporting us without breaking any rules.

When we are open to receiving these signs we will start to see them and recognize them with greater frequency. The first step is to accept them as signs and not just as coincidence or something that just happened. When we accept them we can then begin to ask why that particular sign was sent and what exactly is it trying to tell us. Where is the sign attempting to lead us or keep us away from? If we just say, "oh that was a funny coincidence," then we will miss the whole message and also be less inclined to see other signs in the future.

These signs are being sent to guide us towards what we need in life or to keep us away from danger and unnecessary risks. I have read many examples of people who follow the signs that Archangel Michael sends to them. He is a protector angel and helps many people. He has been known to urge people to change lanes, slow down, and speed up or all kinds of messages and they then in turn are saved from a terrible car accident or other incident. The signs can also be comforting and show you that everything is going to be alright.

I have an example of signs from my own life that I would like to share. It was just over a year ago in December 2015 that I was laid off from my last job. A couple months prior to this I was already thinking of quitting as I was not happy there. I had aspirations of creating an online course and had signed up for a course that would teach me how to create my own course. This course was to start in January of 2016. When I got home from work after being laid off I went online and checked my email. I had got an email saying that they decided to open the course a month early and that it opened on that day. The course that was going to help me start a business, just happened to open the day that I got laid off. To me that was a big, flashing, neon sign telling me I was exactly where I needed to be.

These signs literally come in a million different ways. They can come when you are driving and thinking about whether you should start a business or not and you pass a billboard that talks about new business loans at a bank. It can come in the form of a song that you hear that is exactly about what is going on in your life at that moment. They can even come from what you may perceive as a random message from a stranger you pass in the mall but that was not random at all. They can come from the clock when you see multiple numbers repeated like 11:11 or 4:44. It is up to us to recognize the signs and then find out what they mean for us. The same sign could have a totally different meaning for two different people.

There is meaning behind every sign that we get. For example if you are going through a tough time and are feeling down and happen to look at the clock and it says 4:44, this means that your angels are around and are there to support you. 444 is a number that is attributed to angels. Also, if you happen to come across a feather or one drops into your lap that is also a sign for angels being present.

Often these signs can come and go so fast that we completely miss them if we are not ready and open to them. We pass billboards so fast, walk by people so fast, and just listen to the beat of songs instead of the message that we literally miss signs all the time. The signs will keep coming but if we are not open to them we will keep missing them. I suggest that every day when you wake up you give thanks for the signs that you are going to receive that day and then go through your day open to receive. Look at the people you pass. Maybe even the shirt they are wearing will have a sign for you. Maybe the homeless guy asking for change outside of your work will say something to you that will change your life. When we walk around consciously aware, instead of just staring at our phones, we open ourselves up for all kinds of experiences and support. We just need to make that choice to allow it in.

I would like to emphatically state that there is no such thing as coincidence. I do not believe in them and we should never write off our gut feelings or signs we receive as mere coincidence.

I do not believe in coincidences because I believe everything is perfect and divine. I believe this world and everything else was perfectly designed and created. This leaves no chance for random or for coincidences. I believe there is purpose behind everything. Even what we perceive to be the least significant events can have meaning if we choose to believe. Just the mere sight of a fox crossing our path when out for a walk can have a meaning behind it. Meeting someone by "chance" that comes into our life and causes it to change greatly is no mere coincidence. I believe everything happens for a reason and that this reason means coincidences simply cannot exist.

If we write off feelings or events as just mere coincidences then we are ignoring the signs and what they have to offer. Ignoring the signs is equivalent to ignoring God and ignoring our soul and our spirit guides. We ignore our purpose, our power and our true meaning for being here. When we ignore the signs we ignore the support we are being offered. Usually people that have turned their backs on this support are the ones who go through life asking "why me?" all the time.

I know this because I lived this way for the first 26 years of my life. I never paid attention to the signs and I didn't believe in signs in the first place. I did whatever I wanted to do whenever I wanted to do it and never thought about the consequences. I never thought about the future and how my decisions were affecting my life and the lives of those around me. I had no knowledge of my purpose or of anything bigger than myself. It wasn't until I accepted that there was more to life and began to search for meaning that my life started to change. I began to grow and evolve and gave meaning to everything that I was doing.

It is this new level of awareness that brought me to write this book. I want to show that if I could go from someone that had no knowledge of anything in this book, or let alone this chapter, to writing the book on it, then you too can make a change for the better. You can start to give meaning to everything you do and help those around you.

I would never have gotten to where I am today had I chose to ignore spirit, my soul and the signs. The signs and the support will become harder to notice if we choose to take this route. Writing things off at just coincidence is the easy way out and allows us to remain asleep instead of waking up to our true power. We can only ignore our purpose in life for so long before it starts to take a toll on our quality of life.

Start by just saying yes and entertaining the thought that maybe, just maybe, you actually are receiving signs from the divine. Maybe you are supported infinitely and maybe there is something better waiting for you. What is the worst that could happen?

All the signs we receive have a purpose and meaning behind them. The signs are also very good at telling us if we should continue moving forward or change paths. If we are meant to not make it somewhere it can be something as simple as losing our keys or running out of gas. Maybe we were going to send an email and our computer stopped working. That is a sign that maybe that email wasn't meant to be sent or that it could be worded differently.

It is important to be aware of what we were doing and what was going on in our minds when we receive a sign. This will help us figure out what is being communicated to us. What were we working on or who were we thinking about? Where were we going and who were we with or supposed to meet?

If these events are not coincidence, then what are they? I feel that the word synchronicity is a much better word to describe what is going on. When you accept that it is synchronicity and not just coincidence you can start to see the bigger picture for your life and the design behind it. This acceptance will fill you with confidence and motivation to keep moving forward.

Synchronicity is when you realize that everything around you is coming together to support you. Everything is happening through you and not to you. Synchronicity is when you realize that you are at the exact place you are supposed to be and at the exact time you are supposed to be there. It is when you realize that the things that happened to you that you thought were bad were actually good and guiding you to where you need to go. They were giving you the experiences you were supposed to have so that when you arrived where you were really supposed to be you would be ready. Synchronicity is knowing that sometimes good things have to fall apart in order for even better things to come into being.

When we accept synchronicity into our lives we allow ourselves to move forward with the support and confidence that we need. Knowing that there is a design and purpose to our lives and everything we do can be very relaxing and calming. It lets us know that we are not in this by ourselves and that we have infinite support available. We begin to realize that whoever designed this is extremely powerful and loving at the same time and wants us to succeed. Everything we need to succeed in life is available to us once we open up to it.

I will give an example of a very special event in my life that helped get me to where I am today. In this example I immediately recognized the synchronicity that was going on and knew I had to act. In my example I definitely took action based on the message I received and never looked back again. I felt an overwhelming sense of emotion. This emotion was not sadness or grief but was happiness and supportive. I knew that I was going to make it and everything was going to be ok. I just had to keep on going.

My experience was early 2013 in February I believe. My friends had asked me if I wanted to go to a "come as you'll be in five years" party and I said yes. The concept is simple, you just show up as the person you want to be in five years' time. I was excited as I had never really thought about who I wanted to be in the future and at this point in my life I was pretty lost. I had just quit my job, the business I was working on got shut down and I had a lot of other changes I was going through as well. It was a major transition point in my life.

As I sat down to think of who I wanted to be I got really excited at the options that I had. I decided I wanted to be a successful entrepreneur who had multiple income streams with at least one of them being a passive income stream. I also decided I wanted to be a motivational speaker for troubled youth to help keep them out of trouble. I have seen my fair share of troubled situations in my life and I know how easy it is for our youth to stray on to the wrong path. This is still a goal of mine and I am much closer now than I was back then.

I went to pick up my friends and we were on our way. I had given no thought as to where this place was, I just knew that it was in St. Albert, a little suburb just outside of Edmonton. As we got closer, I started getting a feeling that I had been down this road before and that I had been to this place before. As we pulled up my feeling turned into fact and I indeed had been there before. I had been there about nine or 10 years earlier when I had to do community service for being in trouble with the law. I believe I was 17 years old when I did my community service there and I was in awe that I had returned to this place.

Part of our night was to introduce ourselves at the front of the room and tell who we are. So there I was giving a speech about how I was a motivational speaker for troubled youth at a place, where when I was a troubled youth, had to go to do community service. The feeling was incredible and everyone in the room felt it as I told my story. I was overcome with emotion. I knew that I was to take this path in life and that this was part of my calling. It was obvious to me that this was indeed a moment of synchronicity. I don't even want to know what the odds are of me ending up back at this place as I am telling people I want to help keep youth out of trouble. To put the icing on the cake, they were doing door prizes and I won a book that was titled "How to Talk to Teenagers." This was one of the first times I got to experience synchronicity and I will never forget that moment.

That is how powerful of an experience it can be when we open ourselves up to receiving signs and support. I knew I was in the exact spot that I needed to be and that everything in my life had led me to that moment to receive that message. I had never felt so much emotion and so much acceptance and support. There was even a police officer that was at this party as well and she came and talked to me after about how my story had touched her. Prior to this, most of my interactions with police were not of the friendly kind. It was amazing. My life took a different path after that day.

It is important to realize that none of this is here by accident. Everything in this world and beyond, including you and I, were created and designed. There is great comfort and power once we come to this realization.

I feel that everything is too perfect to have happened by a mere accident. It has to be by design and on purpose. When you look at the odds that all the right conditions for life to flourish would come together on this planet at the perfect time by mere chance you will agree that it wasn't by chance. Someone or something or whatever you want to call it designed this and designed us. We are too perfect and the world is too perfect for it to be any other way. There is perfect balance in the world and in the cosmos. The outer reflects the inner and the above reflects the below. Everything is in perfect harmony and meant to be.

When we are able to accept this fact we will be filled with a confidence and energy we haven't felt before. We will feel an infinite level of support and belonging. The fact that someone would go to such effort to create all of this for us to have the experience that we are having right now is pretty incredible. How can we not feel at home and supported when we look at it from this perspective. It is the ultimate act of unconditional love and we can only be in awe of it. We can take much comfort out of the fact that this was all created for us to grow and evolve and that we are here for a reason.

There are also many times where signs will be sent to us in our dreams. When we are asleep and dreaming is when we are in the closest state to the spirit world that we can be. This is why signs are sent to us when we dream. It is when we are most susceptible to receiving them. I believe that the dream world is closely related to the spirit world. It is much easier for them to reach out to us there than in physical reality. There have been many case studies done in this field by a Dr. Michael Newton detailed in his books. For this book, I just want to plant the idea that this is a very popular time to receive messages from the other side.

Our dreams are not random by any chance. Everything that happens to us in our dreams is sending us some form of message. Who we were with, what we were wearing, where we were and even the time of day. There are so many factors that contribute to what the dream is attempting to show us. I just want you to realize that each dream brings a message with it and is not random or just a fun dream. There is a reason you had that dream.

The problem with messages in dreams is that most of us

forget our dreams as soon as we wake up from them. This is a big factor in whether we will get the message or not. I recommend that everyone start a dream journal. It is just something you write your dreams in when you wake up so that you do not forget what they are about. I like to use the notepad in my phone for this. As you write them down more and more, you will begin to remember them with more frequency. This will aid you in finding the message behind them. It would be pretty difficult to find the message if you can't even remember the dream.

The signs that are being sent to us can come from other sources than just the spirit world. The Earth itself and the environment are constantly sending us messages too. As I mentioned earlier just by a certain animal crossing your path that can be a sign. Even if a storm is approaching you that can be a sign that there is also a storm coming in an area of your life too. If you keep on hitting red lights it could be a sign that you need to slow down or you are going the wrong way and should consider changing paths.

Even the stars and what is going on in space can be a reflection of what is going on with you. This is where the saying "As Above So Below" comes from. This means that what is above is just a reflection of what is below and that the two are symbiotic. They are the same only on a different scale. It is easier to look above and see what is going on than to look at what is on the same level as us. If we are willing to take this as truth, then we can begin to receive support from the stars as well.

This is much the same as the people in our lives. It is easier to look at other people and find what we love and hate about them, than it is for us to look in the mirror and find the same. Just like the stars and the environment around us, the people around us are constantly sending us messages too.

The people in our lives and around us are the biggest reflection of us in the world. We cannot see something in somebody else if we also do not have that within us. When we see beauty in a supermodel it is because we also see beauty in ourselves. When we see anger in someone it is because we also have anger inside. Other people just reflect it back in an obvious way to us. Everything we see in others is also in us or we would not be able to see it in others.

This is one of the biggest and most important signs we can receive. When we do see anger in someone it is important not to judge them or ridicule them. We must step back and ask ourselves, "when do I get angry like that?" If one of our friends is always late to meet us we should ask ourselves, "when am I always late?" As we begin to ask these questions of ourselves we build a bigger awareness of ourselves. We will make changes when we see how these traits in others affect the people around them and we decide if that is how we want to affect others too. There are huge lessons to be learned when we begin to look at others in this way.

Our bodies also love to communicate with us and send us messages. Every pain in our body, every injury, cough, cold or flu has an associated message that goes with it. Every disease we ever encounter also has a message with it as well. Louise Hay has written a wonderful book called "You Can Heal Your Life" that has documented this in great detail. For example, she says that if you are experiencing upper back pain it could be because you feel unloved or not emotionally supported. It could also be that you are holding back love from others too.

She says that when we get these messages from our bodies that we can begin to heal our bodies by dealing with the emotional factors that contribute to our pain. By healing our emotions we will begin to heal our bodies too. There are definitely elements of trust and faith at play here as most people go for drugs and surgery and things like that when not feeling good. I would suggest starting with reading the book and working on small things like headaches and coughs and colds before trying to heal big things. Her book is definitely worth the read.

I also want to point out that everything is merely energy vibrating at different frequencies. It is pretty common knowledge in the world of physics and science that everything is energy. Solids, gas, liquids and everything is just matter vibrating at different frequencies. Water is the perfect example. When it is ice it is vibrating at a low rate and when it is gas it is vibrating much higher. We are the same. Someone who is full of hate and goes through life being rude and dishonest is just vibrating at a low frequency. Someone who acts out of love and goes through life helping others and looking for ways to give back is vibrating at a higher frequency.

We have all experienced the extremes of each and know that this is true. We know how it feels when we are in a rage and we know how the opposite feels when we have done something to help someone that was in need. We know each side of the spectrum and we know that love is a much higher vibe than fear and hate. When we do feel down, angry or alone we can choose to vibrate higher by doing something for others or even just by thinking of a time we did. It is as simple as flipping a switch when it comes to choosing what frequency we want to vibrate at.

Every frequency will have its own distinct pattern. This is just how I talked about in Chapter 1 about the water crystals and their different patterns depending on what they were exposed to. Energy and frequencies work in the same way. There is a science called Cymatics that deals with this. It studies the patterns of frequencies and how different frequencies can affect our health. They have done studies that emit different frequencies on sand to show the different patterns. The results are pretty amazing.

This leads me to my next point. I believe that the fingerprints of creation are absolutely everywhere we look. These same patterns I mentioned above are seen repeatedly everywhere in creation. Sacred Geometry shows us the patterns used for creation itself. The Fibonacci sequence shows us how at scale we are all the same and grow following the same patterns.

I call these patterns the fingerprints of creation because to me that is exactly what they are. Whoever created all of this for us left their mark and it is there for all of us to see. We were all created with the same patterns and even nature and all of its creations are no exception. The stars, planets and everything in space follow the same patterns as well. Once we know what the patterns are, we are able to see them everywhere we look.

Sacred Geometry has been one of my favorite things to research in the past few years. It has been about four years since I first discovered it and I absolutely fell in love with it. The Flower of Life is one of the main symbols and it can be found throughout the world in all kinds of different ancient cultures. There is the Fruit of Life, the Seed of Life, Tree of Life and other important symbols that can be found everywhere we look. Even when we are first conceived as one cell and then divide into two cells and again into four and eight cells we follow the pattern of the Flower of Life. It is quite remarkable and amazing to see the cells and Sacred Geometry next to each other. A simple Google image search of "Sacred Geometry Cell Division" will show you exactly what I am talking about. It is much easier to understand when you see the picture.

The Fibonacci Sequence is another amazing pattern that can be found anywhere. Many of you might have heard of it from a popular movie "The Da Vinci Code." The code goes that the preceding two numbers added together make up the next number in the sequence. So for example to start the code it is 0,1,1,2,3,5,8,13,21,34,55,89,144 and so on. This sequence of growth can be found throughout all of nature and even in our own human bodies as well. The three sections of our fingers follow the 3,5,8 code and the same 3,5,8 is found in our hand to forearm to upper arm. This pattern is found throughout nature as well. A pinecone and many other seeds follow this pattern. When viewed from above it follows the 1,2,3,5,8... pattern perfectly. This is seen everywhere in nature around us.

To end this chapter on the signs I would like to say that everything is divine and absolutely perfect. It can be no other way. Everything has a purpose and everything has a meaning.

This includes you and I and it also includes the trees, animals, stars and everything we see. We are each perfect and divine beings and the same goes for every one and thing. The signs we receive and the patterns that are found everywhere we look are the perfect reminder of this. The perfect reminder that we are where we need to be and that we are here for a specific reason and not by accident. That is a wonderful realization to come to and I hope I have helped you see this wonderful connection.

Chapter 9 – God

"You are the Universe but society teaches limitation."
Alan Watts

God is one of the most highly debated subjects of all time. For me the existence of God is no debate at all. If you are reading this far into my book then you already know that I believe there is a higher power greater than any one of us. A higher power that created us and this reality we inhabit for a purpose. Everything is too perfect and exact for it to have happened by chance. There have been far too many reports of people dying and coming back, with stories of the afterlife, to not believe in a creator. There are too many reports of Angels and Spirit Guides and other phenomena to not believe that God is there. For me, there is a mountain of evidence everywhere we look that points to a creator.

So who is this God and what is he doing? I do not for one second believe that God is a person at all. For simplicity sakes, I will refer to God as a he or she alternatively in this book. I believe God is much bigger and grander than what could be contained in a person or soul. God is everything and anything. It is like the saying goes that man was created in God's image. Meaning that we all contain a piece of God within us. I also believe that everything else was created in God's image too. The stars, nature, animals, water and anything we can think of is all God and God is all of that.

In the Bible it says that when Moses was talking to God through the burning bush he asked God what his name was and he replied "I am that I am." I believe the answer to who or what God is lies in these words. Everything we look at, we feel or experience is God. No matter whether we perceive it to be good, bad, warm, cold or anything else, that is still God. Most importantly, I believe God is love, or to put it in a better way love is God. Unconditional love for everyone and thing. There is no greater power or feeling in the universe and nothing that can overcome true, unconditional love. That is all there is. Just sometimes we have to experience hate in order to know what love really is. Like the saying goes "The sun wouldn't feel so special if it wasn't for the rain, joy wouldn't feel so good if it wasn't for pain."

I feel that it is very important that we all realize that we were created in God's image and that makes us very much like God. I would even go as far as to say that we are all God. We all have the same power and same potential within us. We have just been taught that God is something that exists outside of us when in reality, God is very much inside each and every single one of us. We are as much God as the stars and the planets. Each one of us makes up a part of God just like each cell in our bodies makes up a part of us. Just like every cell in our body contains our whole DNA structure, each of us contains God. It can be no other way.

It is up to us to choose to see ourselves in this way instead of how society teaches us to view ourselves as separate from God. We have infinite potential and infinite power within us and we are more than capable of achieving anything we set our minds to. This is not just a fairy tale told to children, it is the truth. It is important to realize that we are God. When we realize this we must not think of ourselves to be more important or above anyone else. When we realize that we are God, we must also realize that so is everyone else.

People have given many names to God over the years. No matter what the name given to God over the years, there is agreement over all people and ages that there is something bigger than all of us out there.

So whether we call God Jesus, Krishna, Jehovah, Allah or any other name does not matter. They are all talking about the same thing. God has also been called the Universe and Consciousness. There are probably a million different names that have been given to God especially when we start to look at ancient civilizations who had dozens, if not more, of their own gods. I just want to make clear that I will only allude to God as God in this book for simplicities sake and as I believe there is only one. One God that is present in all of creation including you and me.

Before we get too far into the God topic I want to state that God has no religion. God exists outside of any of our man made paradigms. We were created in Gods' image and not the other way around. God is present in religion, but they do not necessarily go hand in hand.

How could God have a religion? She predates any known religion by thousands, if not millions of years. God has always been and always will be. Religions, on the other hand, come and go like the seasons of the year. God loves all of us equally and unconditionally. Religion teaches that some are above others and that we are not equals. Religion is a control mechanism and God gave us free will to do as we choose. Religion and God are actually quite far apart from each other and even when religion ceases to be, God will still be here.

God can be found through religion though. I do not want to sound like I am saying that religion is a dead end road and to abandon ship as soon as possible. Many people have found their way and continue to find their way to God through religion. I just want to say that religion is not the only way to God and that God and religion are two totally separate ideas. You do not need to be religious to know God and yet you can be religious and know God. God is everywhere and in everything and eventually we will all find our own way back to him.

As I mentioned in the previous chapter on the Signs, God's messages are everywhere waiting for us to receive them. Ideas we get when we feel inspired, the dreams we have, the people we cross paths with and so much more. Even the way the words in this book are speaking to you is a message from God. It isn't a coincidence that of all the books in existence you decided to pick this one up. Just think of all the things that had to happen for you to even be aware of this one book. It is quite astonishing when you think about it. Just remember we have a choice to take everything as a sign from God or to take nothing as a sign.

Remember we just need to slow down and silence our minds in order to be able to receive the messages.

God will never stop sending us messages or give up on us. So it does not matter if you are 15, 30 or 80 when you are reading these words. At any point in our lives we can choose to slow down and receive the messages. They will still be there. We will keep getting the same message over and over again until we finally get it. This is why we have events or themes that are constantly reoccurring in our lives. God is sending us a message and wants us to learn the lesson associated with that message. If we do not learn the lesson it will keep coming back until we do. The opportunity to grow is always there if we choose to take it.

God left her fingerprints everywhere on creation. Throughout the whole universe we are able to see the same patterns, shapes and forms. On every level from the microcosm to the macrocosm the prints are there. The way our eyes look when magnified are very similar to the way galaxies and the universe look. The arrangement of a small seed is very similar to the arrangement of forests and jungles. One small drop of water acts in the same way as the whole ocean does. Even the people of the world are all unique yet, at the same time, are all the same too.

I mentioned in the previous chapter about Sacred Geometry and the Fibonacci Sequence. These are God's fingerprints out in the open for us to see. How many of us are willing to accept this and see it for what it is? I know for many people it is a huge stretch to accept or to even entertain the thought that it could be from God. It was tough for me to do too. For most of my life I did not believe and it is only until recently that I have begun to take a different perspective. When I did start to look at things from a different perspective, the things I looked at became different. It was like I was seeing them for the first time again and it was beautiful.

God is also the source of energy that fuels this reality that we live in. The same source of energy that connects us all to each other and to everything else in existence. This is the same energy that we draw on for inspiration, motivation and for life itself. God is in the breath that gives everything life.

The world and the universe, just like cars, need fuel or energy to be in existence. Even the sun is burning energy all the time and will eventually burn out. Where do these massive objects get such grand amounts of energy from? It can only come from one place. God. Of course, science will argue that it comes from this kind of reaction and from these kinds of elements but where do they come from? Where do they get their energy from? Where did "The Big Bang" get its energy from if there was nothing in existence before it? In my opinion it all comes back to God. God is the source where all other energies get their energy from. It can be no other way.

I am sure that if you are reading this book that you have heard people, and even scientists, say that we are all connected. The term "we are all one." What is it that we are connected by? That feeling we get when we meet someone that is going to be a big part of our lives. That feeling we get when someone close to us has passed on. There is an energy that flows through all of us and through all of creation. This energy is as much a part of God as we are. This is the energy that connects us to her and to everything else. This is why some people are able to feel what others are feeling and why we get those gut feelings about other people and situations. Why our pets are able to feel when we are sad or when it is time to go to the park. Our pets are probably even more in tune to this field of energy than we are.

This same field is what gives us the energy to stay up until 4 a.m. working on our dreams and goals. This same field is what gives us our second wind in the last five minutes of the Championship game and allows us to push forward. This same energy is what gives us life and gives us excitement and joy. This energy comes to us through the breath and this is why conscious breathing is so important to living a healthy lifestyle. God gives us life and energy through every breath we take. We are connected to everyone and thing through our breath. This is what we have in common with all of creation.

I believe that the greatest gift that God gave to us was free will. Free will is such a great gift because it allows us all to experience life and God in whatever way that we see fit. It allows us to be, do, and have whatever we want. What could possibly be a better gift than free will? We are free to choose whether we believe in God or not. We are free to choose who we become and how we treat people and the world. We are free to choose our sexual orientation and religious beliefs. We are free to choose how we look and where we live. We are free to do anything we want and that is true freedom at its very core. What an amazing gift to have.

People often ask the question "If there is a God then why doesn't he come down and get rid of war or disease?" Free will is the answer. If God came down and wiped out war then would we really have free will? If God came down and eliminated poverty would we really have free will? The world is in the way it is because we have chosen it to be. Through all of our actions and how we treat each other. We have the choice of what kind of world we want to create and this is the world we have chosen. It is up to us and not God to change it.

The beautiful part about free will is that it is always there. If we do not like our results we can make a different decision. If we do not like how we feel we can make a different decision. If we do not like how we look we can make a different decision. If we do not like where we live we can make a different decision. If we do not like the state of the world then we can make a different decision. We can always choose to be, do or have different things. They are just a decision away.

Free will is why I do not believe in the 10 commandments or the reckoning or judgement day. How could a God that gave us free will tell us how we are to use that free will? How could God give us free will and then say but don't use it like this? Free will is free will, we either have it or we don't.

That is why God will not sentence us to spend eternity in

"hell" when he was the one that gave us free will in the first place. We are all doing the best we can with the current level of evolution that we are at. We are all at different stages in life and on different journeys too. I truly do believe we are all doing the best we can at this stage in our evolution. When we learn and grow and evolve we change our beliefs and behaviors and look back at how silly we once were. It is like the old saying goes "if I knew then what I know now." With this knowledge to put things in perspective then how could there be one set of rules to govern everyone if we are all at different stages.

As I just said, we all grow and evolve and thus change our beliefs and behaviors. As we progress through life and through many different lives we will continue to grow and evolve. This is the beauty of having a soul. What we once did and thought was ok we will see in a different light when we have a different experience. We will no longer want to act in old behaviors when we see what that does to others. We will grow and evolve to the point where our beliefs and actions are noble. Whether this takes years or decades or even dozens of lifetimes does not matter in the grand scheme of things.

I would like to mention that God is always with us and would never leave us to be alone. God is always with us especially in the times where we feel alone and like nobody cares about us. God has sent angels to always watch over us and be with us. I have already discussed in this chapter how there is an energy that is God that connects everyone and thing. That is one way in which God is always present. We are all also connected to the Spirit World through our souls and this is the most dominant way in which we have a connection to God.

There is an old story in which God and someone recently deceased are looking back on the deceased man's life and he notices something that he wants to ask God about. He points out that it seemed there were always two sets of footprints walking along in the sand when things were good. His own set and that of God. But he noticed that when things got rough that there was only one set of footprints. He asked God why he would abandon him when he needed him most and God replied that he never abandoned him. At those moments when things were rough was when God carried him forward. I believe this story is the perfect example of God's love for us and what he is willing to do for us. It shows that no matter what, we will never be alone.

There will be times when you feel alone or afraid and not sure what to do next. It happens to everyone and is almost impossible to avoid. These are the times where we need to make sure to take the time to reconnect to God. Connect to that source energy and let it fill us with love, courage and companionship. Taking time to recharge when we feel down is very important to helping us move forward.

I have often heard people ask the question of why God created us in the first place. To put it simply, God created us because there is a big difference from knowing what you are to experiencing what you are. God knows that it is love but how can love experience itself as love if love is all there is? For example, if we were all candles and we were at the sun how could we distinguish one another from each other? All we would be able to see is light. Now if you were to take one of those candles out of the sun and place it in a dark room then that candle could experience itself as the light. That candle would not know itself as the light unless it was placed in an environment that had no light.

This is why God has created each and every one of us. How could God experience herself as God unless placed in an environment that was not God? It would be impossible to feel that or experience that if God is all there was. We experience this kind of problem all the time in life. When we know something but do not feel it or have the experience of it. It is like hearing someone talk about how awesome it is to see the Great Pyramids of Egypt for the first time. We can watch videos and hear people talk about it as much as we want but it will never compare to when we actually experience it for ourselves.

Since God is absolutely everything there is in existence then you can see how it would be quite difficult to experience all parts of herself in one lifetime. This is why there are so many of us all experiencing life in different ways. This is why God gave us free will. Each of us was created for a specific purpose and no life is more important than the next. God needs each of us just as much as we need her.

We each have our own purpose and mission for our lives. For my own life I feel that I am here to help others become aware of who they truly are. Someone like a famous athlete could have the purpose of bringing joy to the world by entertaining. We each have our own journey. Each journey eventually leads back to the same place, yet take different lengths of time and different paths to get there. Even though we are each different parts of God experiencing itself, we all have our identity as well. We each have our reason for being and for coming here.

We all agreed to come here and have these experiences before we came here. None of us were forced to come here or are forced to come back if we do not want to. I know this can sound pretty out there, especially if you are new to the topic. However, it is my experiences in life that have led me to feel this way. All I can offer is my opinion based on my beliefs and experiences. Deep down inside you will know whether or not it resonates as truth for you or not. If you really think about it though, what could possibly be a greater journey than to pretend that you are not God and then end up finding your way back to being God?

I would also like to mention duality. Duality is having two things that are the same, yet different based on perspective. Take up and down for example. If you are on the ground and you look at a tree you say that the leaves are up. If you are on the balcony of a building next to the same tree you would say that the leaves are down. You are talking about the same tree and the same leaves, yet describe them in a different way. Hot and cold work in much the same way. In the summer when it is 10 degrees outside I say it is cold, yet in the winter when it is 0 degrees outside I say it is warm. It is all based on perspective. Right and wrong are the same too. Someone that is well off could say that stealing for whatever reason is wrong, yet a poor person that steals bread to feed their starving family says that it is right.

Duality exists so that we are able to experience the opposite of what we are. This is how God is able to experience herself as being the light when all that exists is light. By creating darkness, or the absence of light, then God is able to feel what it is like to be the light. This is why there must be good and evil in the world. How could we possibly know what it is like to be good if we do not know what it is like to be evil? How could we be able to feel love if we have not felt fear? Duality serves a very important role in our lives and in all of creation.

This is why we do not feel ourselves to be God in the first place. In order to feel and experience that we are God, first we need to experience what it is like to not be God. That is exactly what we are doing here on this planet right now. Every single one of us is pretending that we are not God. When we steal, cheat, lie and do wrong to our brothers and sisters we are experiencing what it is like to not be God. This is the magic of duality. Once we have experienced the ways in which we are not God then we will begin to come back to experiencing what it is like to be God.

This will be a very special time in our lives and will be very rewarding. We will begin to see things differently than before. See the other side of the duality of things. This process of experiencing what isn't and what is God is played out over several lifetimes and will not happen in just a few years. We will go back and forth for a time until we make that choice that we no longer want to experience what it is like to not be God.

There will be some sure signs that will let us know to keep going in the direction we are going. One big sign for me has been that I want to eat less and less meat. Once we understand that we are all connected and are one then how could we possibly want to do harm to another life? When we understand that how we treat others is how we treat ourselves how could we want to kill another sentient being just to please our taste buds?

Another sign could be that you are now allowing more people to get close to you and allowing love into your life. The choices you make will be more rooted out of love than fear. You will be conscious that you have a choice in the matter. Chances are that if you are even reading these words that you are on your way back or that you are at the very least becoming aware that there is more to life than you have previously believed.

When we arrive at this point of our evolution life will start to feel different. We will manifest our goals and desires with greater ease since we will be going with the flow of life instead of resisting it. We will be happier and be able to enjoy life more as we are giving back and helping others as much as we can. We will be full of energy and a zest for life as we will be closer to the source of that energy. We will be more fulfilled and life will take on a new meaning.

Whether you believe in God or not does not matter to me. I did not write this chapter to convince you one way or the other. I wrote it in the hopes that you find something to help you move forward. In the hopes that you gain a better understanding of life and how it works and that it allows you to help others as well. Even if it just helps you get out of a difficult situation then I will be happy and grateful that I could help.

I would like to end this chapter in the same way that I started it. With a quote by the amazing Alan Watts. "You don't look out there for God. Something in the sky. You look in you."

Chapter 10 – Balance

"The major work of the world is not done by geniuses. It is done by ordinary people, with balance in their lives, who have learned to work in an extraordinary manner."
— *Gordon B. Hinckley*

I have talked about what I believe to be the four major areas of our lives in this book. Mental, Physical, Emotional, and Spiritual. I do not believe that one area is more important than another area. All four are equally important and should be treated as such. We cannot give the Physical aspect the most importance and attention and expect to live a balanced, healthy life. This is what most people, including myself, look to do when looking to get healthy.

We must work on each area consistently and with the same enthusiasm and determination as the others. If there is one area that we choose to ignore, it will manifest in the other areas as well. For example, I used to never want to do any work on the emotional aspect as I thought that was just for women. One way this would manifest in the physical form is through ankle injuries in soccer. At first glance one might think what does an ankle injury have to do with ignoring the emotional aspect of life? If you look up what Louise Hay says about ankle injuries you will see that it has to do with inflexibility and guilt. Guilt is a very strong emotion. She says ankles represent the ability to receive pleasure. It would be very hard for me to receive pleasure if I am feeling guilty and not dealing with that emotion. This was the universe's way of telling me to deal with that emotion or the injury would persist. I had ankle problems for two and half years. I always had to wear an ankle brace when playing soccer and then it got so bad that I was wearing a brace on both ankles. I now have been playing without a brace on either ankle for almost two years. Do the work and your life will heal itself.

There are many results we can expect to receive when we do the work in each of the areas consistently. Being able to play soccer without a brace is one example. Of course this will be different for everyone but we can all expect to benefit by doing the work. We can have more energy, happiness and motivation. We will feel fulfilled, on purpose and like we are making a difference. Our relationships with others will transform and we will attract the kind of people we want to be around. Our relationship with ourselves will change and we will be more comfortable in our own skin and with being alone.

Each of the four areas are connected to each other. They have an effect on each other and are not totally independent of each other. In fact they are quite interdependent. What happens in one area will most definitely spill over into another area or multiple areas. This goes for both positive and negative work. For example, someone that exercises a lot will have the tendency to have mental strength as well as it takes a lot of willpower and the right attitude to get results in the gym. Energy moves between all the areas and as you start to do the work you will notice how the work you do in one area will benefit you in another.

This is why it is so important to be consistent in all of the areas. When you start to lose balance in one area it will be felt in one of the others. For example, when I start to eat too much junk food and not fuel my body properly, my mind starts to get weak and I start making excuses for not doing my work. I start to procrastinate and just put things off until tomorrow. When I do not meditate at least weekly I start to have a short fuse and find myself being impatient and quicker to resort to anger. These are just a couple examples of how one area can affect the others.

Balance is just as important in the cosmos as it is in our lives. The conditions must be just right in order to keep everything in harmony. Even if the moon was just 5% closer than it is now, the Earth would be completely different and would not be able to sustain life. If the Earth were to be a little further away from the sun our environment would not receive the right amount of sunlight or heat in order to sustain life. Any little change in the balance of the cosmos and life as we know it would change drastically.

The same goes for the balance of the conditions here on Earth. There needs to be the proper balance in order for life to exist. If the polar ice caps were to all melt, a lot of the land we currently live on would be under water. If we keep on losing trees at the rate we are currently losing them we will see drastic changes in our air quality. Our food supply is being cut all the time with how we keep on polluting the oceans and other fresh water sources. We are walking a fine line here on the planet right now as we are beginning to shift the world out of balance. We can heal this imbalance but it will take a lot of work from everyone.

The balance we have as people between each other is just as important. We will not be able to come together and heal the world if we do not have the proper balance with each other. We must be able to see each other as equals and treat each other with love. We must begin to see the similarities in each other instead of focusing on the differences. We must be ok in spending time alone to recharge and go inside for inspiration. We must stop putting people on pedestals and worshipping them as if they are better than the rest of us. We are all equals and part of the same family. Until we begin to act like this then we will be out of balance in our relationships with each other.

I feel that many of us know what it is like to live a life without balance. This is called chaos. Our society has most people living a very fast paced life. We are always on the go. Going to work, taking courses to advance our education, recreational activities, keeping up with television, the news, and trying to get ahead in life. There are so many more things as well, especially once children are thrown into the mix. When we are in the midst of a chaotic life it is very difficult to slow down and think of your options of how to get out of it. We are so caught up in the storm that we cannot see anything but it.

Most people do not know what a balanced life even looks like. As I just mentioned, we are so caught up in the storm that we cannot see anything else. Even our role models for society on television and movies do not lead balanced lifestyles. The family sitcoms are full of drama and chaos because that is entertaining for people and makes the networks money. How many times do we see celebrity drug and sex scandals? I am sure there are some celebrities living balanced lives but these are not the ones the media focuses on as that doesn't sell magazine copies.

I also feel that given the choice, almost everyone would choose to live a balanced life over a life of chaos. This is a very safe assumption to make. I know there are people out there that love chaos but most people would choose balance. Who wouldn't want to live a life where they could have happiness, health, free time, and love? These are just some of things that a balanced life can help you get. First, we must become aware that we have a choice in what kind of life we get to live. When we are aware of this we can start to look for ways to get out of the storm.

Disease can be one of the worst effects of living an unbalanced life. I feel that there are more than one cause to any sort of disease. I do not believe that we can simply just put it to bad genes or to hereditary cause. Yes those can definitely play a role but if we take care of ourselves properly we can balance out those causes. When those causes are mixed along with being unbalanced mentally, physically, emotionally, or spiritually then we can really start to get sick. This is why so many people often find themselves sick all the time. I see people around me who exercise all the time and are very specific about what they put into their bodies, yet are still sick all the time and never know why. There are symptoms and causes that they are just not aware of.

Disease is very good at showing us where we are at in life. The problem is that many of us never think of it that way. We are always just looking for the quick fix or the pill we can take to make it go away and ignore what it is trying to tell us. I have already mentioned Louise Hay but will briefly mention her again. She says that every disease or ailment has a message for us. I told you earlier how my ankle problems were in part due to being inflexible and being guilty. All other physical problems and ailments have similar messages to give to us and I cannot stress the importance of looking up the work done by Louise Hay to find the message your body is trying to send to you.

Once we are able to hear this message then we can really get down to the cause and more importantly to the solution too. As I said, once I started working on why I was feeling guilty and not able to receive pleasure, my ankles also started to heal. It did not happen overnight and I also did not leave it up to just doing the work. I did use my brace all the time to make sure I would not make it physically worse. I did not take a chance on that just doing the emotional work would solve all my problems. At the time I was not even aware of Louise Hay but I was doing the work. So it is important to have balance in the solutions to our problems as well and not put all our eggs in one basket.

When we live an unbalanced life it seems like we have no control and it is hard to find direction. Life is throwing so many things our way and it can be difficult to stay focused on what we want to do to move forward in life. Everything is out of order and our priorities are not set straight. There are distractions galore that cause us to keep falling into more resistance as it seems we are never able to make any forward progress.

When resistance and chaos are mixed, it can be too much to handle. This is when people start to give up as the combination seems like an impossible mountain to climb. It is important to ask for support in these kinds of situations. Never try to climb the mountain alone. When we go at it alone we just come up against more resistance. There are people that are further up the mountain than we are that are willing and able to help us move forward.

Going from a chaotic life to a balanced life is not an easy transition. If it was easy everyone would have done it. There are challenges and roadblocks that will cross your path and test you to see if this is the path that you actually want to have. In my own journey I came across several roadblocks and I am still not at the balanced life I am striving to get to. Some of my roadblocks were people I care about telling me I can't do it and that I shouldn't even try. Another one was loneliness as when you start to change your life the people around you also change. A sense of not knowing and being afraid of the unknown was a big one for me. This is where I just had to have trust that I was being led to where I wanted to go. Each person will face different challenges and we must remember why we started the journey in the first place to keep us moving forward.

When we start on this journey it is important to take time out and make a plan. Why are we wanting to make change in our lives in the first place? What is that we want to be different and what are we willing to sacrifice? A big part of my sacrifices was drinking alcohol and smoking cannabis. These were a huge part of my social life and when I first quit I felt lonely as I had not replaced those social aspects in my life yet. It is important to set specific goals with timelines of when we want to achieve them. Write them down too. Writing things down in our handwriting has a power that is able to magnetize things to us. When we are done making a plan it is important to put it somewhere that we are able to see or to look it over frequently to keep it fresh in our minds.

When we are done making our plans it is important to review it and look at the parts that we will need help with. Then we must look at the people in our lives that can actually help us achieve them. If we feel like we can do it all on our own then we haven't made big enough plans. We have left an aspect out or ignored one of the key areas in our lives. We must remember that part of living a balanced lifestyle is having open and loving relationships with others. Maybe we know someone that is really good at making plans and putting pen to paper. They could be a good person to start with for asking for support.

I feel that one of the biggest benefits that comes with living a balanced lifestyle is the peace of mind and the sense of belonging. The way you feel about yourself and where you are at in life. The sense of comfort and knowing that you are being infinitely supported. The ability to be able to deal with what life throws at you and keep moving forward instead of taking steps backward. You will feel better and be healthier. Your energy will be lighter and cleaner. People will start to magnetize towards you and want to be around you. I am just starting to scratch the surface here too. The possible benefits are endless and it is up to you how far you go.

The great thing about these benefits is that you get to share them with the world. Even the ones that are personal, like peace of mind, can be seen by others. The more you display traits that others want, people will eventually come to you and ask you how you do it. As people see you make changes in your life and notice how they have affected you, they will start to ask questions. This is when it gets really fun because you are now able to help other people. You are now the one helping others to climb the mountain and get to where you are. This in itself can be one of the biggest rewards waiting for you.

You can start to reap the rewards of doing the work immediately. You will not have to wait until you are at the top of the mountain to feel better. As I said, I am not where I want to be yet but I am definitely seeing and feeling the results. I do not get down and out when things do not go my way because I know I have the tools to deal with it. I have more open, honest and supportive relationships as I have been willing to put myself out there and ask for what I need. My body definitely feels better as I have been fueling it with what it needs and cutting out the garbage. Over the past few years when I run into people I do not see often, they often compliment me on how healthy I look. One of the benefits I felt the fastest was an awareness that I can be more than I already am and that I am capable of getting there.

Consistency is the best way to get to a balanced lifestyle. It is very important to do the mental work first when striving to have balance in your life. I feel this way because your attitude and willpower are what will keep you moving forward. There will be days and even weeks when you just don't want to do the work. This will be when willpower and the right attitude will come in handy. These are the days that will be the most rewarding too.

When we push to do it when we thought we couldn't will let us know that we are capable of more than we thought. This is why mindset is the first chapter of this book.

Consistency means that we do not go too long without working on each area of our lives. Some areas will be easier to be consistent in than others depending on our lifestyle. For me doing the physical work is the easiest as I have two soccer games and one practice every week. I also have a dog that I walk every day. The emotional work doesn't come as easy as it is still foreign to me and I usually only do it when I go to seminars and classes. I have begun to do more at home by journaling and writing things down. This is definitely where I need the most work in to reach balance. I would say to strive to work on each area at least once a week at a minimum until you find ways to incorporate it into your life more frequently. This is a good way to start.

When you come up against resistance or things get chaotic you know that you are losing balance in one of your areas. Keeping balance is very similar to having a car that you want to keep running in optimal conditions. You want to perform regular maintenance on your car. You will want to replace parts that are not working with ones that are. You will also ask others that are more informed in certain areas for their opinions even if it is just to get a second opinion. There will be warning signs in life just like there are warning signs from your car.

We should all be able to take the time a few times a year to reflect and see how things are going. I would recommend doing it quarterly with the change of each season. I feel like when the seasons change is the perfect time to reflect and make changes of your own. Are you where you said you wanted to be three months ago? What is working and what is not working? Are you ignoring certain areas and only focusing on other areas? Are you climbing the mountain alone or have you asked for support? There are many ways to check how well you are balanced in life.

After doing this check up on your balance you can then

decide if you want to make changes or keep going the way you are going. You will not always need to make changes as sometimes things will go your way and you will be doing everything right. It is still important to do the reflections in these times too as something small may slip under the radar of the all good things going on. That small thing may manifest into something big later on. Be consistent with the maintenance of your balance too.

The last way to check on your balance can be the easiest way in my opinion. How many people have you enrolled into your life? How many people in your life know what you are doing and what you are working on? How many people are helping you reach your goals and how many people are cheering you on? Life is so much more fun and rewarding when we enroll other people to join us on the adventure. Things flow so much easier when we get people to help us too. Two minds are better than one. Ask for support.

Your body will give you plenty of signs as well. Anything from headaches to physical injures to the common flu and to more serious diseases can be warning signs as well. Friends and family often give us feedback as well. They will be the first to notice when things about us change for the better or worse. It is important to hear their messages without getting offended. They care about us and just want us to know what they have noticed. It is important to pay attention to these signs and take care of the problem before it becomes too serious.

There are more areas of our lives than just the four that I talk about in this book that we can apply the law of balance to. Like I said earlier, balance is a universal law that governs all of existence.

It can be almost impossible to live a healthy, balanced lifestyle if our finances are in chaos. Even if we have millions of dollars but it is all out of balance and order we will still have high stress levels and no peace of mind. Finances play a huge role in the society we choose to live in and we must be in control of them or they will control us. Debt can be a vicious master of which it can be very hard to escape. Balancing the check book is an important part of leading a balanced lifestyle.

It is also important to balance how we spend our time. Spending too much time working or too much time playing games or being entertained can be bad as well. When we spend too much time working we miss out on the fun of life and we miss out on the important people in our lives. When we spend too much time on entertainment we neglect to take care of business and making sure everything else is taken care of too. It is important to find the right balance between work and fun.

Balance in our relationships is crucial to being able to be happy and get the most out of life. When we have relationships that are balanced, it can be a wonderful blessing in life. What does that look like though? In a balanced relationship there is trust, open communication, respect and love. This goes for any kind of relationship and not just a primary one. This can be for family, friends, co-workers or anything else. There must be an equal give and take in relationships too.

Having a win/win attitude in relationships is the perfect road to take on the way to having balance. Win/win is very different from a compromise. A compromise is when both parties sacrifice something and do not feel like they are both winning. Usually one, if not both, feels like a loss. In a win/win both parties feel like they have won in the situation and can walk away happy. You both work together to find a solution and keep going until one is found.

An example of this could be when a couple are deciding on what movie they want to watch. One wants to watch a romance and the other a comedy. A compromise could be that they decide to watch a romantic comedy and neither really gets to watch what they wanted. A win/win could be that they watch both movies even if one is that night and the other the next night. This is a very basic example of the difference between a compromise and win/win situation.

In order to have balance we must also realize that we cannot possibly meet all the needs that another has on our own. We must allow them to get their needs met from relationships with other people. People must have more than one relationship with people or else they become too dependent and that is a recipe for disaster. It is important that we have more than one person to turn to and that these people understand that fact. Maybe one person is really fun and another person is a shoulder to cry on. Different people meet different needs and we must respect that in order to have balance.

I feel that yoga is the perfect way to check how well we are balanced in life. Yoga is all about balance. Whether you are just a beginner or an experienced yogi you will require balance in yoga. Yoga is a great mirror for our lives. There are days when I get on my yoga mat and some poses are easy and there are days where the same poses give me problems. This is because of what is going on in my life at the time. Even as I progress in yoga and certain poses, like a headstand, get easier I know it is also in part due to how well I am progressing in other areas of my life too.

Yoga not only helps me in the physical but it also helps in the mental, spiritual and even the emotional. This is why it is such a great tool to check our balance. I already mentioned how all the areas of our lives are connected energetically and what happens in one area will spill over into the others. By doing yoga, we simultaneously do the work in all four areas. This can be extremely beneficial and convenient. The perfect place for people to start that might have time constraints in their lives.

Yoga is literally one of the easiest things to start to do to create balance and can be one of the most rewarding things you will do. I know for me that yoga has created flexibility in more than just my body. It created flexibility in my life and spirit. Opened me up to new experiences and feelings. There is so much that yoga has to offer us if we are willing to open up to it.

Balance will not be something that happens overnight.

However, we can take steps every day that will move us towards balance. Every step will bring us that much closer and will bring with it rewards and other treasures. The important thing is to keep moving forward especially on the days when you feel like giving up. Those will be the most rewarding. Then as we continue to move forward we will see the changes in our lives and most importantly we will be showing others that change is possible. It is important for each of us to be that light that shows everyone else the way. Be the change you want to see in the world.

Conclusion

As I said in the introduction, this was meant to be an introductory guide for people wanting to start a journey towards living healthy, balanced lifestyles. I hope that by reading this book you gained some valuable information and tools that will help you on your journey.

You may now be asking yourself what now? I know that for myself after I am done reading a book, I usually just place it on the shelf and move on. Sometimes I will remember some of the information and use it in my life but, for the most part, as time passes I forget what was contained in the book.

I do not want this to happen with my readers. I know that the journey towards living a healthy life is a long one and will not happen overnight or even in the time that it took to read this book.

This is why I have developed a couple projects to help keep people connected and engaged. This way you can keep the concepts of the book fresh in your mind and connect with others that are on the same journey as you. Having other people to connect with and share stories is a golden resource.

First, I have started a Facebook group called "Life Balance Community" that is for people who have read the book and want to stay connected. You can find the group by clicking on the link on my Life Balance book website. It is a place where people can share what has and what hasn't worked for them and I will also do "FB Live" sessions there discussing topics from my book.

The second project that I have developed is an interactive, online course based on my book. This will be a course that will take you through the concepts in my book and give you assignments to help you integrate them into your life.

I feel that experiential learning is much more effective than just reading a book. It will help you truly live the concepts of the book and help make them a part of your life. Like I said earlier, I usually just put a book on a shelf after reading it and just move on in life. This course will make it possible for you to really apply what you have learned and make real, lasting changes in your life. You can also find a link for this course on my Life Balance book website.

I hope you had just as much fun reading this book as I had writing it. It was definitely a one of a kind experience which had its many ups and downs, just like life does. I got to learn a lot about myself through this experience and I hope that you also learned a lot about yourself.

I am always open to receiving feedback and you can do that by visiting the Life Balance book website. Thank you for reading this book and for taking steps to live a healthy, balanced lifestyle.

Stay Free. Stay Curious.
Rodo.

ABOUT THE AUTHOR

Rodolfo Menjivar is an Author and E-course Creator. He was born in San Salvador, El Salvador in the middle of a civil war and soon immigrated to Canada. His family moved to Canada so that he could have a better chance at making a difference in the world.

His greatest accomplishments have come from working on himself. He has dedicated a great amount of time and money to his own personal development. He is always aiming to become better than he was yesterday. He is always enrolled in classes to learn about himself and others and how to overcome obstacles and challenges. By learning and striving to always be better, it allows him to lead others who want to travel down the same path.

He now helps people by leading by example and sharing all the valuable information that he has learned. He believes that being a student is not enough. One must take what has been learned and share it with others so that they too can move forward in life. Rodolfo does this by creating content where people can learn about health, business, leadership and other related subjects.

Rodolfo is also involved in giving back to the community. He is constantly volunteering and looking for ways to give back. Rodolfo is best known for thinking outside the box and carving his own path in life. He is known to not follow the mainstream way of doing things and instead creates his own more efficient, simpler way of doing things.

Made in the USA
San Bernardino, CA
15 March 2017